THE

CIRCLE

BLUEPRINT

Decoding the
Conscious and **Unconscious**
Factors that
Determine Your Success

Jack Skeen | **Greg Miller** | **Aaron Hill**

WILEY

Published by John Wiley & Sons, Inc., Hoboken, New Jersey.
Published simultaneously in Canada.

For general information about our other products and services, please contact our Customer Care Department within the United States at (800) 762-2974, outside the United States at (317) 572-3993 or fax (317) 572-4002.

Wiley publishes in a variety of print and electronic formats and by print-on-demand. Some material included with standard print versions of this book may not be included in e-books or in print-on-demand. If this book refers to media such as a CD or DVD that is not included in the version you purchased, you may download this material at http://booksupport.wiley.com. For more information about Wiley products, visit www.wiley.com.

Library of Congress Cataloging-in-Publication Data is Available:

ISBN 9781119434856 (Hardcover)
ISBN 9781119434849 (ePDF)
ISBN 9781119434863 (ePub)

Cover Design: Wiley
Cover Image: © Barcin/Getty Images

Printed in the United States of America

10 9 8 7 6 5 4 3 2

Contents

About the Circle Blueprint System

The **Circle Blueprint** is a revolutionary life improvement system that is designed to help you on your path to happiness and success. It's made up of three components:

PART 1: THE BOOK. *The Circle Blueprint: Decoding the Conscious and Unconscious Factors that Determine Your Success* by Jack Skeen, Greg Miller, and Aaron Hill delves into the theory behind the system. It zeroes in on four developmental areas—*Independence, Power, Humility,* and *Purpose*—that combine to make you a "whole" and balanced person. Importantly, the authors explain the real meanings of these four words. (You might be surprised to learn their meanings have gotten lost over time.)

The authors paint a vivid picture of what these concepts look like in the life of a person who has mastered them (and conversely what they might look like when you haven't). They give you the language to *finally* understand on a deep level what's wrong in your life.

PART 2: THE ASSESSMENT. This scientifically validated psychometric self-assessment tool reveals your inherent personality traits as they pertain to the concepts in the book. It tells you exactly where you fall on a "mastery" spectrum in the book's four developmental areas—unearthing exactly where you are limiting your greatness. This is the self-awareness piece that truly sparks change and pushes you to move toward balance, wholeness, and a life in which you thrive. By the way, your results are 100 percent confidential, so you can feel free to be completely honest when you answer the questions.

PART 3: THE SUPPLEMENTAL WORKBOOKS. These four workbooks are filled with step-by-step instruction to help you master the four key developmental areas. This is where you "do the work." Some people choose to engage a coach during this phase, though it's not required.

Here are seven benefits of the Circle Blueprint System:

It's incredibly comprehensive. It covers a broad spectrum of behaviors and works well for many different personality types. Also, it sparks improvement (often dramatic improvement) in both the personal and professional areas of your life.

It's personalized. Many self-help books and programs are "one size fits all." They give generic advice on what to do without first showing you where you are on your journey *right now*. (This is why most don't work.) Thanks to the thorough and accurate assessment, the Circle Blueprint System is all about YOU and how you view yourself. Then, depending where you fall on the five-point mastery scale—whose levels range from "hanging on" to "thriving"—you're directed to the appropriate starting point in the appropriate workbook. You start where you are.

It's private. Sometimes people feel uncomfortable revealing personal information about themselves. That's why the system is designed for privacy from beginning to end. Participants are reassured by the knowledge that their assessment results and all subsequent improvement work are completely confidential.

It's flexible. You can read the book first . . . or jump right into the assessment . . . or take the assessment in stages as you follow the book. You can focus your efforts on mastering one of the four developmental areas or all of them. You can take advantage of specialized coaching if you like—or you can work on yourself without engaging any outside help. You can go as deeply as you want and move as quickly as you want.

It's cost effective. While it is beneficial for many people, coaching is *not* required. Once you've purchased the materials you're fully emancipated to work by yourself, at the cadence that appeals to you.

It fosters rapid improvement. Once you become aware of your weaknesses you can improve very, very quickly. It's not unusual for a person to move from "hanging on" to "thriving" in the blink of an eye.

It's a pathway to lasting change. Again, "awareness" is the magic key. Once you know *exactly* what your problems are—what's holding you back from having the life you want—you almost *have* to address them. You know ignoring them is only hurting yourself. And once you see and feel the improvements in your life, you'll do anything to keep from going back to where you started.

For more information about the Circle Blueprint System, please visit www.thecircleblueprint.com.

Foreword

This book is all about becoming a happy, balanced, thriving person who lives a meaningful life. Not coincidentally, this is the kind of person who makes a great leader.

Interestingly, the heart and soul of leadership have not changed in the past 50 years. I have found that the qualities and traits that create the kind of person who inspires others to follow and brings out the best in them are the same qualities and traits they've always been. In an age of dizzying change, I find it very reassuring to know that some things remain steadfast!

As a private equity investor who partners with companies to support long-term growth, I am incredibly interested in the subject of what great leaders look like. In fact, I will invest only in companies whose leadership teams are made up of balanced, thriving people.

It's my belief that no organization can thrive over time, financially or otherwise, without a subset of fundamentally good people at the top, people who care about those they work with and sincerely want to help develop them. The deep-rooted goal of such leaders is to build a strong business that serves the customer, the employees, and the owners—and they wake up each morning with that in mind.

In his classic book *Good to Great*, Jim Collins writes extensively about getting the right people on the bus. By this, he means leaders who are humble but also driven to do what's best for the company. Collins's book is a wonderful, empirically based work that explores how to use these "right people" to create great companies. It's a valuable resource. But what Collins doesn't really address is how to develop the leaders themselves.

That's where *The Circle Blueprint* steps in. Where Collins veers "right" into the business side of this topic, Jack Skeen, Greg Miller, and Aaron Hill veer "left" into the personal development arena.

Becoming a balanced "whole person" starts with self-awareness. In my experience, most people really aren't self-aware. That's why I'm pleased to say that this thoughtfully organized book; the proprietary, scientifically validated assessment; and the accompanying workbooks are all aimed at creating that self-awareness—a necessary first step to becoming a great leader.

The program then provides a very specific framework to help leaders move on from their new place of self-awareness and work to become balanced, fulfilled, successful human beings.

This framework is quite comprehensive, and in my mind that's what makes the program unique and valuable. Too many leader development programs are random, scattershot, and generalized. When you're a leader participating in such a program, you really don't know where your "problem areas" lie and therefore can't possibly know where to focus your improvement efforts.

The Circle Blueprint approach measures the right things, gives specific feedback on how you're wired and how you can best align to the world around you, and offers practical guidance for moving forward on your journey. Plus, you can start from exactly where you are in terms of both how well you've mastered the crucial elements of the Circle and where you are in your career.

When I saw the four developmental areas that Jack, Greg, and Aaron focused on in their book—*independence, power, humility,* and *purpose*—I was quite pleased. They resonated with me in terms of both my own journey and the qualities I see in the leaders I work with every day.

I also like that they get to the heart of what the traits and concepts really mean. Over time, the perception people have about these words has shifted, and most of us have the wrong idea about their original meaning.

Take *independence.* People think it means being self-sufficient— able to pay your bills, make your own decisions, forge your own destiny. But what it really means is being totally free from the need to please others or win their approval. You're free to do what *you* believe is right, not what someone else thinks is right. This is a rare trait, but it is essential to being a great leader.

I have found that when people lack independence, they also lack self-confidence. They can't act decisively. Such people might be good managers, but they can never be great leaders.

The authors say that if you don't possess true independence you'll never be able to tap into your true *power.* This is another area where most people lose their way. They focus on the conventional definition, which centers on attaining and exerting power, rather than seeking to discover it within themselves. True power should be viewed as your own unique, special skill that makes you good at what you do.

We all have a power center. Some people find it. Others never do. And still others find it and use it in destructive ways. While often powerful, these folks are not great leaders.

Next comes *humility*. Many leaders struggle with this area. They seem to have a fundamental misunderstanding about how leaders "should" behave and present themselves. People in my generation tend to think that leaders must be dominant, commanding figures.

I have found the opposite is true. The leaders who inspire the most confidence in others are those who listen five times more than they speak, who don't have an overinflated view of their own importance, who don't mind admitting they don't have all the answers.

The fourth developmental area is *purpose*. I believe that in most instances, this is more of a personal trait than a corporate one. Purpose-driven for-profit enterprises are rare. On the other hand, there are many leaders who have a strong internal sense that they are working toward a purpose greater than themselves—and these leaders are quite powerful.

In the past, a company's "purpose" was usually discussed in the context of making money. However, this mindset has shifted a bit over the last couple of decades. The most successful newer businesses like Apple, Amazon, and Uber are built on the notion of addressing a human need in a new way—a purpose envisioned by someone who saw the world differently.

I'd like to close by saying that this book comes at the right moment in time. There is a growing need for great leaders to help organizations navigate the tumultuous waters of today's marketplace and economy. And for individual leaders there is also a great need—to perform well and improve quickly.

The reality is that we can no longer wait until we're 50 years old with a lifetime of experience under our belt to operate at the top of our game. Things simply move much faster now, and expectations are much higher. And that's why the program described in this book is so valuable—it gives companies a way to know how their leaders are developing and gives leaders a set path to follow as they forge ahead on their journey.

This is not just a business issue. Far from it. It's a matter of physical, emotional, and spiritual health as well. In the middle of so much uncertainty—with the old ways and old rules giving way to new paradigms and new ways of working and living—we owe it to ourselves to become the best, happiest, most fulfilled, contented, and successful human beings possible.

We all know people who are financially successful but unhappy and dysfunctional. Yet the good news is that we live in a time of ever-increasing awareness about the value of happiness and peace. More and more people are realizing that *enduring* is no longer enough. We deserve better. No matter where we are in our careers, we want happy lives, healthy relationships, and a sense of purpose and meaning.

We owe it to ourselves and the people around us to not merely survive but to thrive—and *The Circle Blueprint* offers us a way to get there.

John M. Goense

Introduction

Are you as happy as you would like to be? Don't think too hard about this question; it's a simple yes or no. If the answer is honestly yes, put the book down and look for something else to read. If the answer is no—not that you're unhappy, just not as happy as you would like to be—then this book is for you. Our guess is that if you picked the book up in the first place you are searching for something more. You might not know exactly what it is, but you hope the "more" is out there and if it is, you want it.

You have been successful...at least to some extent. You have probably worked hard at life. You may have a good education. Perhaps you have risen to some level of leadership at work, or raised a family, or put away some money for retirement.

But do you ever ask yourself, "Is this all there is?"

We have asked thousands of people one very simple question: "Are you thriving in your life?" We use the word "thriving" to describe a life where nothing is missing, where you have it all. Thriving doesn't mean you are particularly wealthy or popular but that your life is rich, happy, and meaningful. Those who are thriving have found the more that others seek. We asked them to choose one of the following descriptions of their lives:

1. I am hanging on by my fingernails. Despite all I have accomplished my life isn't good at all.
2. I am eroding. I'm not desperate but my life is a grind and does not seem to be headed in a positive direction.
3. I am treading water—just sort of enduring my situation. My life isn't bad, but I would not say it is good, either.
4. I am growing. My life is on a positive trajectory. Certainly, it could be better, but I am reasonably satisfied and optimistic about the future.
5. I am thriving. I am creatively engaged in my work and life. I am at the top of my game. I feel energized, balanced, healthy, and happy.

Approximately one-third were reluctant to choose a response because the question itself made them uncomfortable. Almost no one chose number five—I am thriving. Most people responded that they were eroding or treading water—enduring their life rather than living it purposefully.

What is true about your life?

We all know stories about people who appear to be thriving. People like Warren Buffett who, at 86 years old and despite his wealth, goes to work every day. You might expect a man who has achieved such financial success to have cashed out and retired to a tropical island, or to have spent at least some part of his wealth on a lavish lifestyle. Not so with Mr. Buffett. He lives in a very modest home—actually the first house he purchased in Omaha, Nebraska. He drives an ordinary car and works in the same office he and his partner have occupied since they started their business. Mr. Buffett does not work because he has to. He works because he wants to. It brings him life. He thrives in what he does.

But, thriving is not only for those who are financially successful. Perhaps you know a couple who, after years of marriage, are still in love. They are thriving in their relationship. Or, people who feel deeply satisfied with their lives, who are making a difference in the world around them. It is not always the rich and famous who live great lives. In fact, more often than not, it is easier for ordinary people to find the pathway that leads to true satisfaction and deep joy.

Marianne Williamson, in *A Return to Love: Reflections on the Principles of "A Course in Miracles,"* wrote:

> *Our deepest fear is not that we are inadequate. Our deepest fear is that we are powerful beyond measure. It is our light, not our darkness that most frightens us. We ask ourselves, "Who am I to be brilliant, gorgeous, talented, fabulous?" Actually, who are you not to be?... We are all meant to shine, as children do.... And as we let our own light shine, we unconsciously give other people permission to do the same. As we are liberated from our own fear, our presence automatically liberates others.*

Williamson speaks to a deep truth; that every one of us has such potential for greatness that it is difficult for us to comprehend or accept. She is calling us to give up our proclivity for mediocrity and to stretch for greatness. As we shine, our light encourages others to shine, as well. Each of us has the ability to radiate a deep joy and contentment while exuding a power more than sufficient to change the world.

It is your right to shine, to thrive, to live a life of purpose and meaning. It is your right to wake up every day saying, "Wow, my life is amazing," and to radiate joy, power, and peace every moment of every day for the rest of your life. It is your right to thrive.

Thriving is unrelated to material success. Does this surprise you? Certainly, we need money to support our lives, but excessive wealth does not add to life satisfaction. Many very wealthy and outwardly successful men and women feel neither secure nor happy. We know of a man who is desperately working toward his goal of building a $100 million nest egg. He claims he will feel safe enough to relax when he has reached that goal. If this is the standard for well-being and security, very few of us will ever experience it. Our friend is looking for security where it cannot be found. Until he looks in the right place—inside his own life—he will live with constant anxiety. If he arrives at his goal, he may discover he feels no more secure, and he may just move the goal to $200 million.

You probably are not worth hundreds of millions of dollars, or tens of millions. Most likely not even a million, or a hundred thousand dollars. You find this story to be amusing, if not ridiculous. But if you make $40,000 a year and think you would be unburdened if you only made $100,000, you are playing the same game. Security, peace, and success are not tied to increased financial wealth.

In his book, *Drive*, Dan Pink observed that thought workers (those who don't work with their hands for a living) are not motivated by money. Once they are paid sufficient money to meet their needs, three things increased their motivation: (1) Autonomy. People liked to have control over how they approached their work and how they did their work; (2) Mastery. People are naturally motivated to improve their skills; and (3) Purpose. People want to feel like their work matters, that it contributes to something bigger than themselves. (Pink 2009) Pink discovered the importance of what we call the Circle

Blueprint: a map of life choices that shape the quality, satisfaction, and impact of your life. We all long to live satisfying, meaningful lives. Money has its place, but it is not the primary driver of thriving.

Thriving is the result of tending to what you put in your Circle and mastering the elements of your Circle Blueprint. All of us have the ability to thrive in our lives but many of us have lost track of the path toward thriving and get stuck just enduring or even worse, eroding or hanging on. We end up settling for less. This book was designed to help you rediscover the path that leads to thriving.

One client said, "Using these concepts helped me understand my unique map, the way I am wired on the inside and how to best align with the world around me. I transitioned out of a career I didn't love and started an entirely new one. Now I am much more successful. I find joy and deep satisfaction every day." Another told us that these concepts helped him find his happiness: "While working through the Circle Blueprint, it hit me one day. I felt a sense of freedom and joy I hadn't felt since I was a kid—well before I worried about being popular at school or stressed about pleasing others with what I did in sports or at work. The funny thing is, it was there the whole time, I hadn't really changed, I just needed to free myself to be happy—and the Circle Blueprint helped me do that."

Our hope is that you will find in this book encouragement and the tools to thrive in your own life. This book is the starting point in a system we have created and designed to move you forward on a path to true contentment in your life. The book introduces and explains both concepts and elements required to create and sustain you on your path. We also acknowledge that a book isn't always adequate to equip you to apply these concepts to your unique life situation. To help you more directly apply the Circle Blueprint to your life, we created the second part of the system: a psychometrically validated self-assessment designed to bring forward your latent dispositional enduring personality traits as they pertain to the concepts and elements of your Circle. Once these areas have been self-assessed, the final piece of the system includes workbooks and exercises created to help you move through each element as you gain mastery and balance in your Circle. This system has been designed to allow you to move through your development at your own pace and in total privacy.

Chapter 1

The Circle Blueprint

What is the Circle Blueprint? The Circle Blueprint is a framework that illustrates the conscious and unconscious factors that determine the quality of a person's life. Your Circle encompasses values, dreams, character traits, causes, people—what truly matters to you. It determines who you will become and what you will accomplish. It defines your purpose and ultimately your happiness and satisfaction.

Everyone has a Circle. Your Circle probably includes people you love, such as family members and friends, or causes you care about, like saving the whales, defending your country, or taking a stand for the rights of others. It might include character traits such as honesty, responsibility, or self-discipline. You may have personal hopes, dreams, or goals in your Circle: finishing your undergraduate degree, working for a certain company, writing a novel, or running a marathon.

In terms of human development, everyone starts off with a small Circle that includes only self-centered values: comfort, safety, pleasure. Infants are exclusively focused only on the comfort of a full stomach, a dry diaper, and a warm bed. As we grow, life challenges us with opportunities to expand our world that require adding new things to our Circle. The "terrible twos" are noted for a push for independence that shows up in endless questions and persistent defiance. Going to school requires following rules, forming friendships, and

1

learning new skills. Adolescence brings the challenge of breaking away from your family to find your unique place in the world. Each stage of life changes the composition of your Circle. New content is added that changes the mix and balance, and other times, content has to be removed to bring balance. Imagine an adult wearing a diaper and having a pacifier in his or her mouth—these items were long discarded, and much as we remove these items from our lives as we grow, we also have to remove items from our Circle at times if they unbalance our Circle. How we negotiate these challenges of adding and subtracting significantly impacts the quality of our adult lives.

By the time we have reached young adulthood, most people—but not all—have expanded their Circle with activities beyond pleasure, self-protection, and other self-focused values. Those whose development has been stunted by trauma or neglect will still prioritize values that are life-limiting. A person whose Circle is filled with activities limited to pleasure, for example, may take drugs or steal without concern for the future or other people. Even those who grew up in healthy and happy homes can fail to fully develop their Circle and, so, they limit their success and life satisfaction. They may have not completed a fundamental developmental challenge, stopped adding new and more meaningful content to their Circle, or failed to keep the elements of their Circle in balance.

Self-focused values such as pleasure and self-protection are not inherently bad. You might listen to music or read classic novels because they give you pleasure. A healthy degree of self-protection will enable you to set appropriate boundaries and avoid dark alleys. But self-focused values are inherently limited in the degree to which they allow your Circle to grow—and when your Circle stays small, your accomplishments stay small. In the same way a child's world expands when she learns to walk, the quality and impact of our lives expand as we increase what is in our Circle and as we balance our Circle.

The ways you choose to spend your time is the starting place to understand the size and richness of your Circle. Everyone fills every

24-hour day with some mix of activities that range from self-centered to other-centered, wasteful to meaningful, and pleasure-centered to cause-oriented. By keeping track of how you allocate your time over a month, you will have a good approximation of the activities you have included in your Circle. But knowing the activities that are important to you isn't enough to determine the true value of your Circle.

People engage in the same activities for a variety of reasons. One person might serve in his community watch program because he wants to make sure his neighbors are safe. Another person might serve because it makes her feel important or for a sense of adventure. The purpose behind our choices can vary from being extremely significant to being petty or even devious. There may be those who serve in their community watch program only to case the neighborhood for burglary opportunities. Hence, not only what is in the Circle but also the values in your Circle are critically important to understand.

The values in your Circle are not wishes or actions, but motivators that lead to actions. The people and causes in your Circle as well as the values you place within your Circle keep your attention, focus your energy, and direct your activity. They are not merely pipe dreams, but dreams that lead to action, expand your Circle, and impact your life and the lives around you.

How you enlarge and balance your Circle makes all the difference in the world.

Many of the people the world considers to be great were ordinary people who created a very big and masterfully balanced Circle. Mahatma Gandhi began his adult life working as a lawyer, but his career was unremarkable at best. He was so self-conscious and shy that he could barely speak in court. People made fun of him and it was difficult for him to find work. When he found a job in Africa, he was deeply troubled by the mistreatment of his people by the white ruling class. His concern for others forced him to expand and balance his Circle leading to new choices. Rather than dressing and behaving like an Englishman, he began wearing clothing from his native country. He regularly tended to his countrymen in the hospital. His Circle expanded further when he realized that he needed to do something that would permanently change the political and social landscape of India. Liberating India from British rule was now the focus of his life. This rather inept lawyer now led a nation in a resistance movement and became a man people traveled the world over to learn from.

Similarly, Martin Luther King Jr. was a gifted preacher, but when he expanded his Circle to include the cause of civil rights for all African Americans, he earned a place in U.S. history as an influential leader. Mahatma Gandhi and Martin Luther King Jr. are not alone—men and women whom the world might view as just ordinary people impact their lives and the lives of others by enlarging and balancing their Circle.

What Is in Your Circle?

Determine the content of your Circle by asking yourself two questions. What do you spend your time on, and why do you make those choices? If you choose to spend 10 hours each week working out in the gym, it demonstrates that something about your physical well-being is important to you. If you spend 60 hours each week working, you have placed a high priority on work.

However, it is not enough to only know how you allocate your time. It is also necessary to know why you make some activities important. Working out at the gym because of vanity is quite a different motivation from exercising in order to promote and protect your health. It is not that one is good or the other bad, but we believe the latter motivation to be richer and more meaningful. Similarly, if you are working 60 hours each week because it is demanded of you, that is far different from putting in those long hours because your work is meaningful to you and you believe it has great benefit to others.

Our assessment—which we will walk you through in later chapters—will assist you in understanding the size and quality of what's in your Circle and the balance of the values in your Circle. If you are interested in using the assessment, we encourage you to do so. It will help you understand where you are now in various areas of your life. Are you hanging on, eroding, treading water, growing, or thriving? We offer steps in each chapter that can help you move forward as you begin your journey to make your Circle bigger, more balanced, and richer. It is only by knowing where you are that you can take the next step toward building an even better and more meaningful life.

Chapter 2

Enlarging and Balancing Your Circle

The Tale of Two Brothers

Two brothers were raised in a middle-class home in a stable, loving family. Both played sports. Both graduated from high school. Both appeared to be living good and meaningful lives and seemed destined to continue on that path. But, appearances can sometimes be deceiving.

In college, the older brother chose to party instead of study. Soon his grades began to suffer and he found himself at risk of failing out of school. He hid his failure from his parents. When he was finally kicked out of school, he pretended he was still enrolled and continued to take his parents' money. His parents took on debt to support him.

When his lie was discovered, he came home and got a job. He really didn't like working any more than he liked studying. He found a girl who liked to work and married her. But she soon tired of supporting him, and they divorced. He moved back home.

Eventually he moved to another town and got a job. His parents hoped he was finally making something of himself. He married again and had two little girls. Unable to sustain success, he lost his job and hid it from his wife. He pretended to go to work but instead hung out with friends. He couldn't sustain the deception for long, though. His wife took the girls and left him. He moved back home again.

7

The older brother was stuck in patterns of self-destruction. His efforts to improve his life repeatedly collapsed in on him. His Circle never grew and was unbalanced.

The younger brother had a much different story. He worked in the summer and applied himself to the job, regardless of the task. He worked hard in sports and was often chosen to be captain of his team. He became good enough at baseball to earn a scholarship. Like his brother and many other college men, he liked to have a good time and party—but he generally did so in moderation so as not to put his future at risk. He met someone, fell in love, married and started their life together. They both got jobs and worked hard. His job wasn't much fun but he knew it was the first step toward a successful future, and he stuck with it.

He and his wife were devoted to their three girls. The younger son moved on to a job with more of a future. He became one of the most successful employees among his peers and was promoted to a position that required travel. Despite being gone from home much of the week, he coached his daughters' teams and attended their school events.

How did one brother get stuck while the other kept growing? What did the younger brother learn that his older brother missed?

Of course, this story is not only about these two brothers. It's about you and me and the people around us. Why does one person excel while another fails? Why does one life stagnate while another is vibrant? Why is one person bitter and resentful, while another is grateful and giving?

We frame these questions in the context of the Circle. Why does one person's Circle expand, while another's does not? The older brother in the story did not expand or balance his Circle. Meanwhile, the younger brother successfully expanded his Circle beyond self-gratification. The balancing of his Circle created character growth, productive work, a partner and family, and a vision for a meaningful life.

Your Life Is Meant to Thrive

From birth, our lives comprise a series of developmental tasks. The successful completion of each task prepares us for the next. The first task was to start breathing. Then we learn to suck, cry, smile, hold our heads up, roll over, sit up, crawl, and walk. These tasks are elements of early childhood development. Health and child care providers as well as parents track a baby's progress toward these tasks as a sign of overall health. If a child consistently fails to meet developmental milestones, it's known as "failure to thrive."

As you mature, the necessary developmental tasks become more subtle and quite profound, such as learning to trust people and to believe in your gifts and talents. Early childhood tasks give way to broader areas of development. Much like failure to thrive as a child, failure to thrive in young adulthood and beyond is similarly associated failure to learn a lesson or master a skill. Your development is arrested when you fail to gain awareness of and take ownership of your Circle. In early childhood developmental tasks are linear—you can't learn to sit up or crawl until you learn to hold up your head. This is true also of the Circle. As a young adult you must work to gain mastery and balance of the Circle's areas of development in a linear fashion, as we will highlight for you in subsequent chapters. The areas of development in the Circle are independence, power, humility, and purpose. Any effort to expand what is in your Circle beyond its current point is limited and/or doomed to failure until you become aware of the Circle Blueprint and work toward mastering and balancing its elements.

Adults who fail to thrive have the small and most unbalanced Circles. They don't value much. Their interests are self-indulgent; their dreams, if they have any, limited to self-protection or pleasure. Their impact on those around them is negative or nonexistent.

Adults who thrive, on the other hand, have learned to expand and balance their Circles by developing their character and cultivating their sense of purpose. Those who grow and balance their

Circles develop personal habits that support a higher quality life. They are productive and make good choices. They find success comes to them and they are a positive force in the world. Before we explain the four areas of development, we first highlight some ways that our Circles grow.

Pleasure

Perhaps the smallest Circle is one that encompasses only momentary pleasure. If that is all that is in your Circle, you will indulge every whim and desire, even if those choices are ultimately detrimental to your own well-being. When pleasure defines all that is important to you, it often leads to addiction, reckless indulgence, and crime. There is little or no capacity to create anything that requires discipline, productive labor, or delaying gratification. Such a small Circle results in a very dysfunctional and unhappy life.

It is only as you expand and balance your Circle that you escape the limitations you have imposed upon yourself. The first step is to include your own well-being in your Circle and remove those aspects of pleasure that are detrimental.

Caring for Self and Your Well-Being

It is fundamentally necessary to include your personal well-being in your Circle if you want a meaningful and happy life. Caring for yourself sometimes requires you to do things that are neither fun nor easy, such as education and/or training for work. In order to succeed in your education, you learn to delay gratification through self-discipline.

Self-care and discipline are the foundation of all future success. They are necessary to a successful relationship, partnership, family life, and career.

Caring for Others: Family, Acquaintances, Friends, and Partners

Throughout life, you develop personal relationships with others—the earliest are usually with your family members. Some people you come to know are merely acquaintances, while with others the relationship develops to where you share a bond of friendship. These personal relationships expand your Circle. Committing to a life partner is a special relationship that creates a huge expansion of your Circle. Until you make the commitment to share your life with another person, your life is your own. Your choices only affect you, or at least, you only have responsibility for your personal well-being. You can be as self-focused as you please. But, when you add another human being to your Circle everything changes. That person's well-being becomes important, and for your life partner, it can become as important as your own. Your time and possessions are now shared. Your decisions impact another person to whom you are responsible and deeply love. You simply cannot successfully have lasting meaningful relationships, particularly a thriving intimate partnership, if your Circle has not expanded beyond your self-interest. And, in growing beyond self-interest, you master the amazing skill of selflessness. Great relationships—whether with your family, friends, or partners—are built on the foundation of selflessness. And, selflessness expands your life immensely.

There are two ways to be in a relationship. The first way is to look out for yourself. For this to work, you only give to the extent the other person in the relationship gives to you, and you take to the extent the other person takes. You must always be looking out for yourself to ensure it feels fair—keeping score by adding and subtracting who has done what to determine the next action to take. The second way is to quit keeping score and give yourself completely to the relationship. You give no thought to what is fair to you and you quit worrying about what you have added and taken relative to the other—you quit playing tit-for-tat and just engage selflessly in caring well for your partner.

The first approach is likely to be fair but comes at a cost: Not only do you spend valuable time and mental resources keeping score and worrying about who owes who and the debits and credits of the relationship accounting statements that could be spent elsewhere, but relationships built on this foundation fall apart as soon as fairness tips out of balance. The relationship is always fragile and prone to rupture.

The second approach frees you from this accounting burden, and the selflessness you give to the relationship is likely to be recipro-cated, enriching your life in many ways.

Imagine taking the second approach to your relationship with the person you choose to share your life with. What if you determined your happiness by your ability to enrich your partner's happiness? It is a bold thing to love in this manner. You are fully trusting that your partner is similarly committed. But loving in such a selfless manner has tremendous benefits.

It is almost impossible to argue in such a relationship. Imagine that you and your partner are going to the movies. Your partner asks you what you want to see and you express your preference. You ask for your partner's preference and the choice is a movie other than yours. You respond that you now want to see the movie your partner selected because you truly want to make your partner happy. Your partner responds by wanting to see the movie you picked because your partner is so wildly in love with you and deeply seeks your happiness. Regardless of which movie you see, both of you are wildly happy. One person saw the movie of her choice. The other was able to bring happiness to his partner.

Moreover, loving someone in this manner changes you for the better. Prior to expanding your Circle you could be completely self-centered and it really did not matter. But, there is no way to have a successful partnership without learning to share and to love. It is unbelievably expanding to learn how to make someone else's interests and needs as important as your own. It makes you a bigger person to learn to stop saying "mine" and start saying "ours." Sharing and caring are skills that get you beyond the limitations of selfishness and self-interest. They open your eyes and heart to the needs of others. They enrich your life with companionship and intimacy; things that are foreign to people only focused on themselves.

Parenting

If you are not a parent, it is likely that you have some understanding of the challenge and opportunity in raising children. If you are a parent, we are confident you know. Life before children is relatively easy. You decide what time you go to bed and when you get up. Your car is as clean and orderly as you like. Your home is quiet and neat unless you choose otherwise. You come and go as you please.

Life after children is completely the opposite. You find yourself up in the middle of the night, bone wearily changing diapers and rocking this bundle of joy. Your car is crammed with car seats and strollers. You can't go anywhere without lugging tons of gear, and the quiet you want at home is now filled with crying, crying, and more crying. What did you do to your life?

You expanded your Circle. You took on the responsibility to care for and nurture a new life. What an awesome responsibility. You created a dream for your child whether or not you realized it. You want your child to have a good life. That might include finishing school, getting a good job, having his own family. Whatever your dream, it motivates you to do what is necessary to make it come true. You change diapers without complaint. You rock your precious child at night without resenting the loss of sleep. You play games that really do not interest you, help with homework that you do not really understand, and attend PTA meetings that are dreadfully boring. You do all you do because you care. Children are the incentive to grow beyond the selflessness of partnering. To be a good parent you must master the skill of self-sacrifice. All good parents actually give up much of their lives for their children. They forgo their freedom. They accept the burden with joy. Self-sacrifice is a game changer.

Work

Of course there are many ways to expand your Circle apart from personal relationships and parenting. There are many people who have not been in a committed relationship and/or do not have children who have very large and rich Circles. Work is another opportunity.

The smallest Circle you can draw around work is to see it only as a means to a paycheck. When this is how you view work, you are only motivated to do the very least necessary to get paid. You do not want to know what others are doing. You are not interested in learning any new skills. By having such a small Circle you have made yourself only minimally useful to your employer.

You expand your Circle when you take ownership of your job and make it very important to deliver an excellent product in a timely manner. With this expansion of your Circle you may stay late, put in time at home, or do whatever is necessary to live up to your internal expectation of success. Your boss can count on you to deliver and so finds you more valuable than your peers who are only doing what is necessary to be paid.

You can expand your Circle still more by taking ownership of the success of the company. While in the restroom of a company we noticed the CEO was picking up scraps of paper towels that had fallen from the dispenser. Many employees had been in that restroom that day and had passed right by those scraps. They did not see it as their job to pick them up. We were impressed that everything about his company was in the CEO's Circle, even scraps of paper towels in the men's room. Every employee can have such a big Circle. When you do, you look for opportunities to collaborate with peers. You want to understand how you can better align to create success for everyone. You pick up scraps of paper towels.

There are many ways to expand your Circle. Well-being, personal relationships, parenting, and work are examples, and are not intended to be an exhaustive list.

The amazing truth is that all of the people we consider to be great are, in fact, ordinary people who drew a big Circle for their lives. Gandhi was a lousy lawyer but when he drew his Circle to include the Indian people, he became a man the world pursued for his power, wisdom, and compassion. Martin Luther King, Jr. was an inner city preacher who, because he drew his Circle around the treatment of African Americans in the United States, became an unstoppable agent of change. You might consider yourself be an ordinary person, but there is no limit to who you can choose to become. It depends only on the Circle you choose to draw.

So, if greatness is available to everyone, why don't more people become great? Why aren't you living as large as your heroes? The easy answer is that your Circle is still rather small. The more complete answer is that you haven't yet wrestled with and mastered the key elements that create a larger Circle. Aristotle said that courage is the one virtue that unlocks all others. We contend and provide evidence that mastering the elements of the Circle unlocks the pathway to mature character. That is why you need to understand your Circle Blueprint.

Truly great people are people of great character. There are countless examples of people who appear to be great but lack character. Quite often, their absence of mature character eventually comes to light and exposes their absence of true greatness. Character is the foundation upon which the building of a truly great life must rest. Character isn't something you can buy or steal. Character comes from mastering core issues that build a powerful and amazing life. Character comes from putting the right things in your Circle and becoming the person you need to be to fulfill those dreams. Character takes time to mature. And, not only do those core issues need to be mastered, they need to be balanced and kept in balance. It is only those who do so who arise to the level of greatness.

Chapter 3

Four Critical Developmental Tasks

It is one thing to become clear about what is and is not important to you. This in itself is a big step toward thriving that few people take the time to do. It is another thing altogether to grow your life into one that is purposeful, powerful, and strong. Growing your Circle requires development similar to the development you took on as a child. In order to thrive in your life, you must work toward accomplishing four critical developmental tasks: gain independence, embrace your unique power, embody humility, and pursue purpose.

There was a time when you were helpless. You could do nothing to care for yourself but cry when you were uncomfortable. You were completely dependent on your caretakers to feed you, clean you, clothe you, and love you. Even turning over was a chore beyond your ability. The best you could hope for was to find your thumb. But, you developed. One day, you learned to smile and smiling gained you the attention of others. You learned to talk and could then ask for what you wanted. This was much more efficient than crying and hoping others could decode your distress. You learned to walk and so could go and get what you wanted without having to wait for others to show up. You learned to use the potty and so could be around other children for longer periods of time. All of these developmental steps were critical to your physical independence. Without having successfully navigated them, your functioning would be severely limited.

Unfortunately, hardly any attention has been paid to the developmental steps needed to create a mature inner life. Without such guidance, many adults remain adolescents or infants at their core. They have mature bodies but immature lives. There are so many manifestations of arrested inner development:

- Adults who make their lives all about themselves. They need to be the focus of attention in almost every conversation.
- Adults who will do whatever is necessary to attain their goals even to the point of violating the rights of others and breaking the law.
- Adults who can't control their temper and rage when things don't go their way.
- Adults who make false statements regarding their accomplishments and achievements pretending to be who they are not.
- Adults who overindulge in substances at the cost of having a productive and meaningful life.
- Adults who refuse to take on adult responsibilities, requiring others to care for them rather than caring for themselves.

Four Critical Areas of Development

There are four fundamental developmental areas necessary for every human being to move toward thriving.

1. *Gain independence.* We all learn to please the important people in our lives in order to get along. It is natural to do so … and it works. We can get a long way by pleasing. But pleasing others by itself will never produce a mature and powerful life. One way to define independence is to think of it as not being concerned with pleasing others. This doesn't mean you are purposefully offensive or insensitive, but that you deeply believe that being yourself and expressing yourself is more important than fitting in to the expectations of the people around you. If you are not independent of the need to please others, your Circle will be limited by this need. Other manifestations of lacking independence are dependence on substances and comparing yourself to others.

It is only when we grow past pleasing that we find our own voice and begin to claim our own lives. This is not an easy step. Many people fail to achieve it. Independence is where most people seem to get stuck. Quite frankly, unless this need to please is mastered, all other aspects of the Circle are somewhat irrelevant if your goal is finally to be free, happy, fulfilled, and leading a great life. We want to help you understand how to navigate past pleasing to find your power.

Independence is about taking 100 percent responsibility for your life and its outcomes. Independence is living with freedom from insecurity and self-doubt. Signs of mastery of independence are knowing your own preferences and desires, speaking openly and candidly in all circumstances, and possessing your life with full confidence and clarity.

Independence should not be confused with separateness from others. Quite the opposite is true. When you have mastered independence you are able to fully experience the joy of others without the need to read their attitudes and wishes so as to fit into their expectations and needs. One of our favorite expressions from a colleague, Jim Dethmer, is "only when you can be you, and I can be me, can we be us."

2. *Embrace power.* When we give up pleasing others as the source of our strength we are quite vulnerable and may feel as if we have neither the skills nor connections to ever amount to anything. However, it is only when we have given up pleasing that we are capable of finding our own source of strength, that which lies within each of us. We have each been given a gift, some special quality or skill that is designed to be our source of power and value in the world. We like to call this quality your "power." We believe that all people have some unique power in them. Some of us have found that which makes us powerful and brilliant at a young age. Others of us know what our power is and have not yet had the courage to embrace it and make it the focus of their

life. Still others have found their power but have not yet integrated it with fully developed Humility and Purpose. They come across like peacocks—more interested in showing off their plumes than in utilizing their giftedness for its best and highest good.

Similarly, some of us become so frightened of the possibility of failing, we abandon our power because we know it will put us on a path that feels risky. It is easy to be ordinary. If you aim low, it is not difficult to hit your target. But, it is our belief that not one of us is intended to aim low. Quite to the contrary, we were given our special gift to aim very high even if doing so increases the risk of failure. Failure is often the sign of courage. It means we were willing to put our gifts to full use. We shouldn't be afraid of failure but of being unwilling to take big risks. It is only when we risk big that we attain things worthy of our life.

Finding your gift creates personal power. Reaching out for something special and testing your power and faith in yourself can be very challenging. Sometimes the people that surround you are eager to see you fail because your failure lessens the pressure on them to find their uniqueness. This is especially true of those who have not yet found their own power. They could be family members, friends, and loved ones. They don't necessarily mean harm. Your effective use of your power may strain the relationship and create an imbalance and insecurity in them. One sure way to know if someone is truly your friend and really cares about you is to notice the reaction you get when you're reaching for a dream or goal. If that person is supportive, you are fortunate to have that relationship. If that individual is not supportive, understand that negative energy is always driven by that person's need to feel secure. Regardless, it is critical for each of us to follow the *best* path for our lives. We must each find, and follow, the power we have been given and achieve the greatest fulfillment possible in each of our lives. Anything less will leave you feeling as if something important is missing from your life. It is our responsibility to find and use the great gifts we were given. Finding and accepting your power is critical to having a truly powerful and productive life.

3. *Embody humility.* When we find our true power, it is easy to fly too high. We can become so impressed with ourselves that it becomes difficult to see how to integrate our gifts with the needs of others. You may have met talented people who are so full of themselves that they have no room for anyone else. It is only when our power is seasoned with humility that it becomes optimally useful.

Humility is simple to understand, yet is often misunderstood. Merriam-Webster defines humility as "the quality or state of not thinking you are better than other people: the quality or state of being humble." For the purpose of the Circle Blueprint we will define humility as having an accurate opinion of your talents, accomplishments, and limitations, while keeping them in perspective. Humility is eliminating your self-focus to the point of forgetting yourself. Humility is achieved by expanding your Circle. The bigger your Circle becomes, the more concerns beyond yourself become important. These bigger concerns become the context for defining how you view yourself. Instead of your interests and needs being the sole focus of your attention, your expanded Circle populates your attention with a multitude of other concerns.

Being humble isn't being greater than you are, nor is it being less than you are. It is being what is true and real about you. If you pretend that you are less than you are by holding back on your gifts and power, you demonstrate a false or pseudo-humility. While this may sometimes be the path of least resistance and the easiest way to get along in your circumstance, you are misrepresenting the truth about you. You are meant to bring your gifts and power to the game of life every moment of every day. On the other hand, when you pretend to be more than you are to impress others or to make yourself look important, you have wandered out of humility in the opposite direction. You have actually sold out your true value in order to pretend to be someone you are not.

Those who have mastered humility know how to live between those extremes.

Those who have mastered humility have gained the skill of forgetting themselves to focus on how they can best bring their true gifts and power to those around them. Thriving requires coming to experience your life as one with others and the world around you. Later in the book we will discuss paths to humility that intertwine with our humanity. We hope to demonstrate that humility combined with your experience of your full power is a gift for the entire world to enjoy.

4. *Pursue purpose.* When we gain independence, find our power, and carry our power with true humility, there remains one more developmental task on the pathway toward greatness. Until we see our lives from the highest point of view, we are limited in understanding our true value. We are all limited by what we see. If we only see a part of the vastness of the world around us, our impact will be limited by our view. But when we see from the highest vantage point, we can see everything. It is from here we will discover our true sense of purpose. Finding your purpose gives you the clarity to know how to be your very best self, to live an extraordinary life.

We believe the pathway to purpose is the cultivation of spirituality. Spirituality can mean many things to many people. For us it means rising above the material. There is much in life that is material. We work to make money that we need to buy food, clothing, housing, and all manner of other necessary things. We save money to secure our future. We spend a great deal of time and effort providing for our material needs both now and in the future. But, we believe life is much more than the material world. When we move beyond the material world, we begin to appreciate the source of such things as love, nobility, goodness, beauty, and kindness. It is only when we are comfortable with the world of spirit and can see our lives in the context of that world that we are able to truly discover our greatest calling and purpose.

We invite you into that discovery because we believe it is absolutely critical for you to discover who you were meant to be.

Each of these developmental steps is necessary to have a truly rich life Circle. Even though it might appear that some can be skipped, in truth they cannot. There are many examples of people who seemed to have very rich lives that one day collapsed in despair and pain because one or more of these necessary elements had not been mastered.

Chapter 4

Balancing the Circle

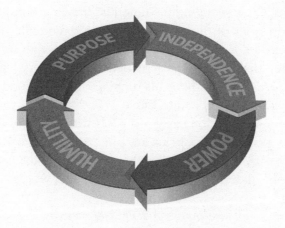

Jorge Munoz arrived in America as an illegal immigrant in the early '80s. He became a citizen in 1987. One evening as he left a bar he noticed all the destitute and illegal day laborers and the flame in his heart was lit. He found out that most of the men sleep under a bridge or in the Elmhurst Hospital's emergency room and skimped on meals in order to send money to their loved ones at home. Since then, he has been cooking enough food to feed dozens of day laborers in Queens, which he delivers at the corner of Roosevelt Avenue and 73rd Street in Jackson Heights every evening at 11:30. Jorge delivers the warm, cooked meals in rain, snow, thunder and lightning. He estimates that he has served food to more than 70,000 people since 2004.

25

*The whole operation is financed from the $600 he receives weekly
for driving a school bus and whatever he secures in donations. On
August 4, 2010, Jorge was awarded the Presidential Citizens Medal
by President Barack Obama.*

—Gerber (2013)

We believe Jorge Munoz is a great man. He may not be the wealth-
iest man on earth nor someone about whom a biography will be
written. But his life is amazingly satisfying and rewarding. He sees
life differently than do ordinary people. Even though he is not by
any means a rich man, he doesn't obsess about his need for more
money. He sees his money as a "trust," a resource given to him to
invest in the world around him. He is not surviving his life. He is
thriving. He is not spending his time just hanging out, getting by or
vegetating in front of the television. Every day is filled with meaning and purpose. He sees himself as a rich man with an abundance
to share. He doesn't see himself as better than others. The homeless
men he feeds are his brothers, his friends. His life is good and strong.
He has a big and balanced life Circle.

Not everyone has done as good a job with their life Circle as has
Jorge. Many people's life Circles are quite small and imbalanced.

This quote by Marianne Williamson provides guidance as to where
we lose our balance. Let's take a closer look at her words.

*It is our light, not our darkness that most frightens us. . . . Your playing
small does not serve the world. . . . There is nothing enlightened about
shrinking.*

Williamson suggests that many of us are "playing small." We are
surviving our lives. Our big vision for our lives is to get the next
paycheck, pay off the next bill, avoid getting fired. We haven't dared
to imagine that we are amazingly talented. We haven't been willing
to consider our light and what we might bring to the world. Is she
not right? Is it not true that you have many more moments when you
live in fear than in dreams of doing great things? Do you not focus
more on your weaknesses than on your strengths? Is this not playing

small? It is only when we are willing to come out of the darkness and to dream a big dream that we will create a big and balanced life Circle.

Williamson writes, "We are all meant to shine, as children do." We agree. We all shined as children. We believed we could be and do anything. We had big dreams. We had hope. We thought we were amazing and invincible. But, somewhere along the way, we lost some of our innocence and faith in ourselves and in life. Perhaps you got bad grades in some subject you didn't like. Or, you were given feedback that you were stupid or not able to achieve. And you believed what you were told and forgot how amazing you truly are. You began to lower your expectations and to settle for a life that was simply okay.

Now, as an adult, you find your life is just that: okay. It isn't great. It isn't powerful. It isn't extraordinary. And, you make it acceptable by reminding yourself that you are like most of the people you know. But, until now, you did not know about Jorge. If he can live an extraordinary life, why can't you? Recognizing the need for balancing seems clear. The question is what do we balance?

The Problem of an Unbalanced Circle

While there is clearly a developmental movement through the four key elements of the Circle Blueprint, it is also critically important that they be brought into a proper balance. When one or more are developed at the expense of the others, a potentially wonderful life will be distorted and will fall short of reaching its potential. An unbalanced Circle becomes another shape all together—imagine an oval when two positions of the Circle take precedent or a crescent moon where full sections are not developed. The Circle might even become a shape possessing a series of indents as if we were drawing a cloud, or it could have a large protrusion as if we were drawing a dialog box from a comic strip. The lack of balance can come in many forms, and so it is important that we balance all aspects.

Power without humility results in hubris. Unfortunately, we are all too familiar with stories of seemingly very successful executives in some of the biggest corporations in our country (e.g., Kenneth

Lay of Enron) who became so attached to their success that they bent the rules, only to find their companies destroyed and themselves behind bars.

Purpose without an understanding of power leads to grand dreams and plans without any effective ability to bring them to life. Being a dreamer is a wonderful thing. But, it only becomes useful when it is harnessed to our unique gifts.

Humility without power and purpose leads to the false conclusion that you are ordinary and have nothing special to contribute to the world. You may be a decent person, but you will miss the reason you have been put on the earth. You won't begin to understand how to shine.

Without independence, it is impossible to find or to grow power, humility, and purpose. Your Circle will be so constricted as to severely limit any further development. This is often the source of bitterness and pettiness in people. They are too afraid of displeasing others to be themselves and they bitterly envy those whose independence has provided them with the opportunity for real power and significance.

As you can see in Figure 4.1, the independence and power elements of the Circle Blueprint are more fully developed while the

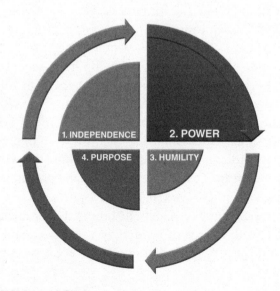

FIGURE **4.1**   **Unbalanced Circle**

humility and purpose elements are underdeveloped. An individual with such a Circle—let's call her Nancy—will have given up pleasing and learned and mastered her power. We imagine she comes across as skilled, self-confident, and driven to succeed. She might be striving to rise through the ranks of the company and to be included on the executive team. Or, she might be an aspiring writer who plans to write the next best-selling novel. But, she has not mastered humility. In fact, it is the least well-developed of her four key Circle elements. Hence, when you are around this young and talented woman you will find that she talks almost exclusively about herself. She loves telling you (and everyone she knows) about her dreams for her success and how she will use the money she makes as she reaches her goals. You might find that all of her dreams for the future are self-indulgent. She plans to buy a home at the beach and a new sports car. She plans to leverage her notoriety and break into a new (and she thinks better) social circles. As she drones on and on, you may find yourself wishing for a way to end the conversation and get away from this woman. She isn't connecting with you. In fact, she shows no interest in you whatsoever. This is the telling sign of someone who has not yet mastered humility. People like Nancy don't see anyone but themselves. And you might notice from her dreams that her purpose element is lacking as well. She has no higher purpose in which she wants to invest. Her success is for her alone to enjoy. She doesn't begin to understand that her gifts are meant to be invested for the good of the world and not just for her own pleasure. Over time, she may become aware of a shallowness and emptiness in her life. These are the symptoms of her imbalanced Circle. Many of us have Circles that are either too small or too out of balance to do justice to the life we were meant to have. As a result, we either have given up dreaming for our lives or have dreams that are woefully inadequate. We spend our lives worried about pleasing our boss, our spouse, our neighbors and friends; we change our behavior and conversations to fit our changing contexts just as a chameleon changes colors to fit its surroundings. We either don't have any idea what our power might be or are too fearful of making a change to invest in that gift that would bring our full power and potential to the world. Or we think either too little of ourselves to be of any use to others or far too much of ourselves to even notice those around us.

To be sure, Jorge Munoz is not the only person who has built a truly meaningful life. It is for all of us. It is for you. Regardless of your current situation, you have the chance to open your eyes to new potential, new opportunities to be a bigger person, someone whose life is tuned in, aware, alive, and vibrant. Jorge drew his Circle around the hungry and homeless day laborers in Queens. He saw an opportunity and wanted to make a difference.

What did Jorge find that so many people seem to miss? There are hundreds of thousands of great men and women around the world who know the answer. Many of their names we will never know. Every night they are off to their second job in order to send their children to college. Every day after school they are tutoring those who need help. They are manning food kitchens, serving in the armed forces, running businesses, and raising crops but in ways that are unbelievably rich. They are happy and satisfied people. They have discovered the true meaning of life. They have mastered the Circle Blueprint.

The good news is that you are never finished drawing your Circle. It does not matter what it was yesterday or 15 minutes ago. You can change it at any time. You might not like how much you weigh and decide right now to put your body in your Circle. You might be bored in your work and decide to put your giftedness in your Circle. Your marriage might be languishing in mediocrity and you decide to put your love and passion in your Circle. You might choose to make a difference in your community. Or, you might simply choose to help a single person or animal in need. Every day you can change the impact and quality of your life. *Every great person is simply an ordinary person who drew a Circle around something big.* Every person who is thriving is doing so because he was able to become intentional about what was truly important to him by balancing his Circle. Your Circle not only changes the world around you but it profoundly changes you—the person who draws it. There is nothing to keep you from having a great life, and we mean that in every sense of the word.

Our intent is to help you understand the size, elements, and balance of your Circle. And, with appropriate understanding and balance to allow you to master your purpose in life and ultimately achieve personal greatness. While there are many common lessons, it is also true that we each have a unique path. What will be clear as you progress through the book is that you can expand and balance your own Circle to become your greatest self.

Balance is not only key to having a Circle that is not distorted, it is also the key to endurance. Your mechanic will tell you that if your car's tires are out of balance they will wear out sooner than they were designed to last. Similarly, if your life is out of balance in any way you will eventually show signs of wear and tear. One of your responsibilities in life is to understand, find, and maintain your balance.

Balance is different for each of us. Some people thrive working 60-hour weeks. For others, that is simply too much. Some people need a lot of time by themselves to recharge their batteries, while some need hardly any. The important thing is to assess your personal balance in every key area of life.

The Circle Blueprint is your way to create a rich and amazing life. It is your opportunity to assess where you are and where you want to go. It is a plan for thoughtfully expanding your impact and the quality of your life.

But, there is more. Some people seem to be more effective at expanding their Circle than do others. In fact, many people seem to get stuck along the way and their lives hardly change at all. Perhaps you have had the experience of going back to where you grew up for a high school reunion and being startled by the group of people whose lives haven't seemed to have changed much from when you graduated. They still hang out with many of the same people from high school and do the same things you used to do so many years ago. It is almost as if their lives have stood still. How does this happen to people?

We encourage you to take ownership of your life Circle Blueprint. The difference between the wise and the foolish is amazingly simple. The wise put to use every good idea they encounter and learn from their own mistakes. Fools, on the other hand, quickly forget the good ideas they learn and go on unchanged, even repeating their own mistakes. We are asking you to be wise today.

If you encounter any good ideas in this book, put them to use today. Take one step in the direction of making your life Circle Blueprint bigger or stronger. Then take another. We believe you can change the world by expanding your Circle, even if only a little. And, we know that if each of us commits to expanding his or her Circle each day, there is no end to the goodness we will create together.

Exercise

Complete the chart in Figure 4.2. Where do you need to make some changes? What would bring you into better balance?

PERSONAL BALANCE

Too Little		Hours at Work		Too Much
Too Little		Time with Family		Too Much
Too Little		Friendships		Too Much
Too Little		Exercise		Too Much
Too Little		Rest		Too Much
Too Little		Play and Fun		Too Much
Too Little		Personal Development		Too Much
Too Little		Food and/or Drink		Too Much

FIGURE 4.2   Personal Balance

Since balance is different for everyone, this exercise may help you identify where your life is in and is out of balance. Look at each area listed in the chart. Feel free to add areas that we neglected to include or to disregard any we included that aren't relevant for you. Put a check in the box that best represents how you are investing your time. For example, if you are a person who needs a lot of time with friends to be fulfilled but you are spending so much time at work that you have no opportunity to be with your friends, you would put a check in the box at the extreme left of the chart for friendships. When you are finished, review where you need to work on bringing your life into better balance.

Chapter 5

Distress and Vision in Expanding Your Circle

In Figure 5.1 you will see that the first step in expanding your circle is having something matter for you; to have a vision, a passion, a drive. The things that matter to you, that you want to improve, develop, and achieve act like fuel that drives the process of growth and change. It is critical that you come to understand how things come to matter or fail to.

Why does one single mom decide to get a second job to put her kids through school while her friends don't seem to do anything to help their children? Why does one employee take work home so he can complete it on time while his buddies simply punched out and went to the bar? Why does Jorge take on feeding the day laborers while his friends don't?

We believe there are reasons the single mom works a second job, and although not entirely the same, reasons that an employee goes the extra mile and that Jorge shares what he has to help feed those with less. The motivation for each of these people to expand their Circle is that it was important to them. It was important enough to the mom to provide more opportunities for her children, to the worker to meet deadlines, to Jorge to feed others with what may be viewed as meager means. For those who do not expand their Circle not much is very important.

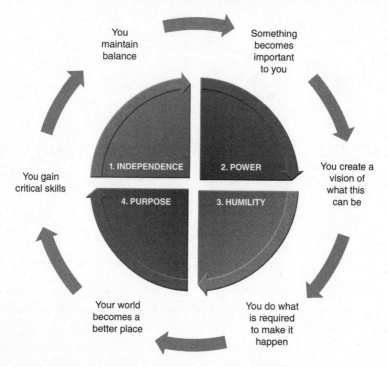

FIGURE 5.1 **Steps in Expanding Your Circle**

How do things become important enough to motivate you to expand your Circle? Everyone has resistance to change. It is part of human nature. We tend to think we have it pretty good and that change will make our lives worse. We tend to resist changing jobs, even if our job is boring. We tend to stay in bad relationships because we are fearful of what change might bring. We tend to persist in bad habits because it takes too much effort to give them up.

Resistance leads to a kind of myopia where our vision tends to narrow and limit our ability to see new opportunities in the world around us. We become accustomed to the status quo. We see only that which supports our current circumstance. Without seeing opportunities, our Circles don't grow.

The Two Levers

There are two levers that can open our eyes to see new opportunities. The first is distress. In many of the stories we have recounted, an ordinary person was moved by distress of some kind. It might be your own distress or that of someone—or something—else. Jorge was moved by the distress of the homeless and poor day laborers outside of the bar. You might be distressed when you step on the scale in the morning, or when you are laid off from your job, or when your relationship becomes so bad that something terrible happens.

It is unfortunate that so many of us depend on distress to overcome our resistance to change. It is only when the pain and destruction in our lives becomes too great to ignore any longer that we are willing to contemplate doing something different.

The second lever is vision. Vision is a much better lever to open our eyes because it doesn't require pain and suffering. When we catch a vision of who we could be or what we can do, it can become great enough to expand our Circle. It can make a change important enough to be put into your Circle. The mother working a second job to send her kids to school has a vision of her children having more opportunity than did she. The worker who takes work home to make certain it is done right and on time has a vision of advancing her career.

Many people enjoy watching the Olympics because the games are filled with stories of young people whose lives have been shaped by vision. Many of them talk of having watched the games as little children and being mesmerized by the gold medalists. They were inspired to buy posters of those people and tape them to the ceiling of the bedroom. Every night they would dream of being good enough to earn a medal. That dream expanded their Circle. They gave up the lives of normal teenagers, spending all of their free time training and conditioning. Then, one day, it was their chance to shine. An ordinary child became a world class athlete because her vision had changed her Circle. Being the best in the world was important to her. And because she made it important, she became the best in the world! Imagine what expanding your Circle can do to your life!

First Steps

Distress and vision are not enough on their own. Change does not occur, nor does your Circle expand, unless you actually take a step in the direction of change. All of our stories have that one element in common. Each person did something. They took action. Until you take action your Circle remains unchanged. Many people have dreams of what they want their life to be, but they never do anything to make those dreams come true. We want you to dream a dream for your life and then make it happen.

This understanding of human change is described in the Change Formula, created by David Gleicher.

D (Distress) × V (Vision) + FS (First Steps) > R (Resistance)

You Create a Vision of What Your Life Can Be

Vision. It reaches beyond the thing that is into the conception of what can be. Imagination gives you the picture. Vision gives you the impulse to make the picture your own.

—Robert Collier

One of the defining characteristics of every Circle Blueprint is a vision or dream of a preferred future. It is the desire to create something (a loving marriage, a healthy lifestyle, opportunities for your children, a stable income, shelter for the homeless) that determines your Circle.

So, what vision do you have for your life? What do you want to be that you aren't now? What do you want to have that you don't have currently? What do you want to do that you aren't doing? What do you want to change? What difference do you want to make? Big or small, any vision for your life that creates goodness, expresses kindness, shows care, or seeks to improve the welfare of others will begin expanding your Circle.

Everything starts with vision. Vision is a tremendously powerful force. It can create almost anything. In the last chapter, you made some notes about areas of your life that were out of balance. We encourage you to have a bigger vision, but as a first step, what about trying to bring your Circle into balance? You have identified areas out of balance—some form of distress—now, if your vision is to balance your Circle, what first steps can you take? We think you will find that this small step toward balance will help you toward the bigger vision for your life.

Chapter 6

Driving Your Circle Expansion: Brakes and Gas Pedals

The Law of Attraction*

There was a time when people didn't understand the law of gravity. That doesn't mean gravity didn't exist. Until Sir Isaac Newton named it, it simply operated beyond our understanding. The same is true of the law of attraction. The law of attraction posits that our thoughts have creative power. Your vision actually creates your life.

This is not a new idea. The field of medicine has understood the law of attraction for a very long time. When new medicines are tested for efficacy, they are given in combination with placebos. Placebos have no medicinal value of any kind. They are made up of benign substances like sugar or salt water. However, when people believe the placebo is actual medicine, many of them get better. Placebos almost always have some healing effect. Somehow, the belief that a substance will make you better creates that result.

Our thoughts shape our lives in ways much bigger than we know. You may know people who are always worried about getting sick and seem to be sick a lot. Do their thoughts somehow attract illness? Jesus stated, "I tell you the truth, you can say to this mountain, 'May you be lifted up and thrown into the sea,' and it will happen. But you must really believe it will happen and have no doubt in

_____
*As discussed in Ronda Byrne, *The Secret* (New York: Atria Books, 2006).

your heart" (Mark 11:23). Was Jesus saying that there is amazing power in belief? Is it possible that you can create almost anything for your life if you can believe?

Brakes and Gas Pedals

If the law of attraction is real, why do so many people live such limited lives? Perhaps it is because we have such little faith. There are many things that limit our ability to believe. Among them are things like resentment, cynicism, skepticism, fear, and doubt. To the extent we are in the grip of such negative forces our ability to utilize the creative power of belief is stunted. These brakes limit our ability to harness the power of the law of attraction in order to build an amazing and powerful Circle for our lives.

The gas pedal is belief. When we cultivate simple belief, we expand our power to create in our lives and in the world around us. When we see the world as full of possibilities and ourselves as full of creative potential, we begin to harness the power of the law of attraction.

How likely is it that you will be a millionaire? For most people the answer is "quite unlikely, if not impossible." You have no belief that you could ever make that much money. Your belief limits your ability to even see a new possibility. However, you know there are people who are making that kind of money. Until you can believe you have that potential, you have no ability to see the road that leads there. This is true not only for money but also for happiness, love, care for others, and anything else that might make our lives wonderful.

Creating a PhD, a Story of Belief

Ted's's first career was in trouble. He was 30 years old, married with two children. He was pastor of a small Presbyterian church he had founded on the East Coast. The church had grown from four families to about 200 people when the trouble started. A minor decision by the leadership ignited a conflict that embroiled the church in a horrible fight. Ted was completely undone. He had no ability to deal with such ugliness and anger. He felt trapped. His dream of being the pastor of that church for the rest of his life was shattered. What options did he have? He needed to support his family, but who wants to hire a minister who failed in his first assignment?

In the middle of the conflict he was sent to a five-day retreat for ministers in southern California. He was reluctant to go. The last thing he thought he needed was introspection when he felt he was under siege. But, the retreat was amazing! It was run by psychologists who were skilled at helping the participants better understand their potential and roadblocks.

Ted was overwhelmed. Suddenly, he had the vision that he needed to become a psychologist. He thought that was a highly impractical dream. At the time, graduate school was extremely competitive and Ted had no credentials. Even worse, he had no money, and a young family to support. The obstacles were insurmountable, seemingly higher than a mountain.

Ted didn't care. That week when he was in California, he applied at the school that sponsored the retreat. They told him it was too late. Admissions would be closed in a week. He still didn't care. He found a place in California to take the necessary admissions examination. He completed all of the forms. He obtained all of the recommendations. And . . . Ted was turned down.

He didn't care. Ted found another school that accepted him that very year. But, he didn't have any money, the school was in Chicago, and Ted lived on the East Coast. What could he do? One of the leaders of the church one day offered Ted $1,500 a month because he believed in him. Ted rented his house and moved. A year later, he reapplied at the first school and was accepted. Ted's vision became a reality! To this day, Ted is amazed by the power of vision.

But isn't this the same for everyone who creates something in their lives? Every sports team creates a vision of winning before it wins. Every couple creates a vision for their family before it occurs. Perhaps every expansion of our lives is preceded by a dream of that expansion.

Write It Down

Exercise

What vision do you have for your life? Take the time to write down everything you want to create in your life. Don't hold back. Don't be afraid. Don't let the brakes hold you back. Write those things down in the belief that you can create anything that is truly important to you, especially if it is built on truth, goodness, love, health, and care for others.

Chapter 7

Creating a Road Map

U ntil you put your vision into words and record it somewhere, it is more likely to remain a wish and to lack the creative power to change your life. Sometimes, we lack the faith to believe we can have what we want and so hold back on expressing our desires. Sometimes, we believe but are too fearful to express ourselves fully. It is only when we get past these obstacles and write it down that we begin to unleash the full potential of vision. This process of writing down our vision is like creating a road map toward the destination of thriving.

Lisa's Story

Lisa had always struggled a bit with the term vision. It seems like the kind of word that belongs to people who use words like "big picture." However, the value of vision became real to Lisa when she went through a divorce.

It seemed that all of her plans for the future were falling apart and would never become realities. The divorce was a terribly depressing time for Lisa and her children.

A friend reminded her that she had overcome a host of obstacles that she encountered in her business career. When problems arose, Lisa was always able to cast a new plan and vision and the business would somehow flourish.

So, at this unlikely time in Lisa's life she chose to sit down in front of her computer and write a business plan for her life. This

45

plan was a path to achieve her desired outcomes for her future. Creating this plan was a challenge because, as a result of the divorce, Lisa would have a lot less money and many new responsibilities to deal with because she would be living on her own and caring for her children.

Lisa found it very easy to write down what was important to her during this difficult time. Perhaps it was because she was finally expressing her needs, even if it was only on a piece of paper. Lisa felt that her lack of showing up and expressing her needs contributed to her failed marriage. Lisa had always wanted to live on a lake in a house that resembled a cabin. She thought it would be great to raise her kids in this type of peaceful environment. She had imagined they would go for walks, go fishing together, and enjoy nature as a family.

But, how could such a dream come true at a time when she had such limited resources? She had convinced herself that this life was only possible if she were living a few hundred miles to the north in Wisconsin or Michigan. Further, she thought she would have to wait until she retired to live this life and that she would need a lot more money than she currently had.

Then a very strange thing happened. Once she had written her dream down, Lisa started to notice that there were several places very much like the place she wanted to live. A few weeks later she found the place she had always dreamed of. And, it was within walking distance of the house she lived in for the previous 10 years! The house she had always desired was right up the street; less than a mile away. It was in need of repair, but, as a result, it was very affordable.

Lisa could not have taken action without first having been clear and honest with herself about her desires. Once that happened the next steps were easy.

Big dreams remain simply dreams until you take action. We have asked many professionals if they have plans for their career, family, marriage, health, financials, retirement, or contribution to society. Most haven't done much planning in any of these areas. They have a vague idea of what they hope will happen, but haven't committed it to any plans.

People who thrive create a blueprint or a road map for what they want to create in their Circle and how they will create it.

Road maps aren't set in stone. You can change them as you move forward. But, they define your destination, your waypoints, and the concrete steps you will take to reach them.

Imagine you and your family were setting off on a weeklong trip. Everyone packs and piles in the car. You start the engine and then realize that you haven't yet determined the destination. You are stuck before you leave the driveway. You have no way to make a decision to turn left or right. No one would do that! Instead, you plan where you are going, the route you will take, and where you plan to be each evening. Now, it is easy to make decisions about your direction, how fast you will go, how long you will stop, and what you will do along the way.

The first action step to make your vision a reality is to create a road map that includes the goal, strategies, action steps, and milestones.

- *Goal:* What is your vision for that area of your life?
- *Strategies:* How do you intend to create that vision?
- *Action steps:* What do you need to do to execute each strategy?
- *Milestones:* Where do you want to be on each strategy and by when?

Accountability

Once you've created your action plan, enlist a person or persons to whom you will be accountable. Alcoholics Anonymous has proven that group accountability is essential for change. For some reason when we share our commitments to change with others, we feel a sense of obligation to live up to them that we don't experience when we only commit to ourselves. Sharing your commitment with a friend or two can make a huge difference in actualizing your intention to change. Share with your friend(s) what you are intending to change and the reason you are doing so. Ask them to check in with you periodically (at least weekly and perhaps daily) to see how you are doing and to encourage you to keep your commitment. Such accountability can be the difference between success and failure.

Chapter 8

Impact on Others

Expanding your Circle changes the world for the better. There are two kinds of greatness in the world. The first is the greatness of ego. Many people seek to be recognized for their accomplishments. They are known because they throw a 90-mile-per-hour fastball, or won two Emmys, or have their name on a building. This is clearly a type of greatness. But, this kind of greatness is built on a weak foundation. So many of those we call heroes turn out to be disappointments when we discover how they achieved their greatness. They cut corners, they cheated, they took advantage of others. This kind of greatness is false and empty.

The second type of greatness is quite different. It isn't about recognition. In fact, many of those whom we consider great aren't recognized at all. They are great because they have chosen to be noble, to put themselves aside and to take on the needs of others. They make the world a better place because of their choices. They demonstrate their greatness in big and small ways, such as:

- Paying for someone's breakfast
- Feeding the homeless
- Coaching their kids' sports teams
- Taking a meal to a sick neighbor

There is no shortage of stories about the greatness of ordinary people who, every day, add to the goodness in the world. Mothers and fathers tenderly attend to their helpless infants. Parents put in long hours at work to provide for the needs of their family. Employees go the extra mile in staying late, lending a hand, training a newer hire. Employers give their employees a second chance to learn a new skill that will serve them in their lives.

The great forces in life are good and evil. Human history is the record of that battle that sometimes seems to tip one way and then the other. Evil is the source of all of the world's suffering. Wars displace hundreds of thousands of people from their homes and slaughter innocent people because they belonged to a certain tribe or nationality. Women and children are sold into slavery for sexual exploitation. People die of hunger or from the absence of clean water while the world possesses the technology to solve both problems. Corporations ruin the environment, threatening our very existence to enhance short-term profitability.

What force stands against the might of evil? Goodness. The world will never forget the image of the courageous man standing in front of a line of battle tanks in China's Tiananmen Square and refusing to move out of their way. The day before those tanks were used to murder hundreds of protestors. His only weapons were courage and the conviction to do the right thing.

Goodness is more powerful than evil. It is only goodness that can protect the world from the horror evil creates. Every time you expand your Circle, you increase the amount of goodness in the world. Your impact is much bigger than you know. Your care for others, your self-sacrifice, your random acts of kindness sow the seeds of goodness in others. The gift goes on and on, often beyond that which you will ever see or know. You may never see all the ripples of goodness that your Circle has created, but you can know that you made a difference and that the goodness you started will continue to expand on and on.

You Change for the Better

One of the most amazing aspects of expanding your Circle is that not only do you impact the world in a positive way, but your life becomes richer. In fact, the most important tool to create a meaningful and satisfying life is to focus on expanding your Circle. The process of creating a preferred future for the objects in your Circle makes you a more mature, competent person.

Maturity is defined as the ability to maintain your poise and constancy of character in difficult times. Think for a moment of the times in your life when you were not able to maintain such poise. Perhaps you can recall times when your felt afraid or frustrated and you behaved in ways you now regret.

I had almost completed my training as a doctor. All that remained was for me to complete my internship under the supervision of a licensed practitioner. I had done well in school, but I had to go into serious debt to finance my education. Now, I had three kids and had just bought a house. I was banking on finally making enough money to get back in the black.

I was killing it as a new doctor. In fact, patients preferred to see me instead of my boss. She was actually losing patients to me. I thought it was great and imagined it was good for her as well since she took a sizeable part of every dollar I brought into her practice. But, it must have been eating at her because during one of our supervision sessions, she made a veiled threat that she was considering firing me.

I was beside myself. What would I do if I walked in one day and she told me to pack up and leave? The patients belonged to her. I would have nowhere to work and no one to treat. I wouldn't be able to pay my mortgage and would certainly lose my new house. I felt like my back was to the wall.

I came in on a Saturday and started copying all of my charts. I knew it wasn't the right thing to do, but I figured if she fired me I would be able to contact my patients and give them a choice of seeing me or staying with my boss. She walked in and caught me red handed.

I was so ashamed of myself. Being scared brought out the worst in me.

Imagine your Circle is so big and powerful that you maintain your composure, sense of self, and power even in the worst of circumstances. This is the goal of a great and noble life. This is our vision for your life. We want you to be so grounded, so confident of yourself, so trusting in the goodness of life, so connected to your purpose that you always see the high road as your only choice in life. We want you to be proud of your choices regardless of your circumstances.

We are reminded here of Jesus' words as he hung tortured on a cross. He had been tormented, beaten, falsely accused, and unjustly punished. As he hung there in horrible agony he prayed, "Father, forgive them for they don't know what they are doing!" Imagine being filled with such grace and love that you radiate forgiveness and understanding on the darkest of all possible days.

Expanding your Circle always requires doing things that are challenging and seem difficult, but the doing of those things fosters maturity.

My friend was telling me about taking his kids into their hot tub when he gets home from work. His little girls are ecstatic with excitement. They need help getting into their suits, finding their goggles and deciding whose special towel is whose. For my friend, the hot tub means the opportunity to slow down and unwind after a hard day. That is not how it goes when he is in the tub with his children. They jump off the edge, so he has to hold their hands to prevent them from banging heads. They splash hot, chlorinated water in his eyes. They step on his feet and unintentionally kick and knee him in sensitive areas. He told me the experience was miserable and amazing all at the same time. It certainly isn't relaxing. But the wonder of his children having so much fun is unbelievably satisfying. The sacrifice of his peace is creating a magical experience for his children and is teaching him patience, kindness, and generosity. He is learning how to make his comfort and relaxation secondary to the experiences he can create for his children. This lesson generalizes to other times they are together and to other people in his life.

The opportunity for greatness is available to everyone. The lessons we have shared with you are simple but the execution requires discipline over a lifetime. This book is not for those who embrace a quick fix or a throwaway culture. Your character defines your ability to grow your Circle. This will take time and will require you to be planful. The good news is that you can start today, right now! Every moment and every day will be a step toward leading a noble, grace-filled, and peaceful life.

Chapter 9

Assessing Your Circle

F igure 9.1 represents how your assessment results would appear if you had fully discovered your power, but had not so completely developed your independence, purpose, and humility. It would also suggest that focusing on humility would be the best place to work on your Circle.

A Circle assessment will show which aspects of your Circle are in balance and which are not. It will provide a guide for you to work toward achieving greater balance on your own timetable with complete confidentiality, freedom, and independence. The assessment and exercises are tools that will unlock your greatest possible self by removing whatever is blocking you from achieving all that your life was intended to be.

Once you have completed the overview, you may wish to take an online assessment that will allow you to gauge the balance of your unique Circle. This process will help you interact with the book and discover opportunities for personal growth.

The assessment is a reliable instrument based on scientifically validated theory that will identify the core issues that are holding you back from having the happy and successful life you seek. We know too many people who spend thousands of hours in and dollars on therapy in the hope of understanding these issues. Having a reliable instrument that can provide this information (think of this like a good bathroom scale for your weight) will make it much easier for you to focus on desired areas where you may be lacking balance. Unlocking

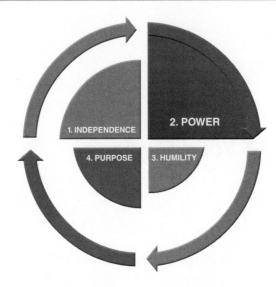

FIGURE 9.1   An Example of Unbalanced Circle—High Power Driven Circle

these issues is the first step toward being able to pursue your personal goals and dreams. Alternatively, as you read through the book, note those areas that are important to you and focus on the steps provided at the end of each chapter. Refer back to these areas as you continue on your path.

Either way, the assessment or simple self-reflection as you work through this book will empower you to take ownership of your life and to provide you the tools to make whatever improvements you want to make on your own timetable.

The assessment first provides you with an overall measure of your mastery of each of the four key elements shown in Figure 9.1. The overview will give you a high-level picture of where you are strong and where you may have work to do. You will learn whether you have mastered one or more of the four key development elements and which ones might require your attention.

Each element of the Circle Blueprint is broken into five or six discrete factors and subfactors. These factors and subfactors provide more detailed information about specific developmental areas of mastery or those that need work.

We all have enduring personality traits that are the result of the mix between our inherited genetics and how we were nurtured. Some of us are outgoing and gregarious, while others are shy and reserved. Some are optimists, always seeing potential positive outcomes, while others are pessimists, seeing what might go wrong. Some are detail-oriented and so make good accountants and doctors. Others are generalists and so are well equipped to see the big picture of where an opportunity might be seized. There are no good or bad personality traits. The combination of our personality traits is what makes each of us unique. And it is this unique combination of personality traits that creates our dispositional tendencies or how we tend to behave in every situation in life.

Some of our dispositional tendencies are called a "manifest quality," which simply means that they can be clearly seen by ourselves and by others. For example, if you are a reserved person, it is highly likely that you and your friends know this about you. Many of our dispositional tendencies are manifest qualities.

Our latent tendencies, on the other hand, are not so obvious. These are our dispositional tendencies that are subconscious or unconscious. Hence, they are not in our awareness and are most often hidden even from those who know us well. Perhaps you have an insecurity about not being recognized for your uniqueness. If so, it might not be something of which you are aware. You may have compensated for this insecurity by not seeking recognition and, in the process, limited your ambition. Or, you might have been bullied as a child and now instinctively respond with anger to those who have authority and power. You might be aware of getting angry around certain people, but be completely unaware of why you do so. It is often our latent tendencies that most interfere with our ability to complete a balanced Circle. It is as if our latent tendencies control us more than we control them. And, because they are difficult for us to see, it is almost impossible for us to develop effective strategies to deal with them.

The Circle Blueprint assessment was designed to measure latent personality attributes for the purpose of translating them into manifest factors for each element of the Circle Blueprint. You may also gain appreciation of these attributes without the assessment if that is more comfortable with you. Either process brings visibility to the underlying causes so that you may introduce an intervention and produce positive change.

The following are examples of why the assessment or self-reflection are necessary to determine an individual's latent dispositional traits as behavioral drivers.

Example 1: Independence and Power-Driven with Low Humility and Purpose

Let's say you are in a meeting with several other colleagues and the meeting is of little or no value for you, and you are providing nothing in return to the other members of the meeting. You decide to get up and leave the meeting before its conclusion. Your Circle most likely reflects either Figure 9.2 or Figure 9.3.

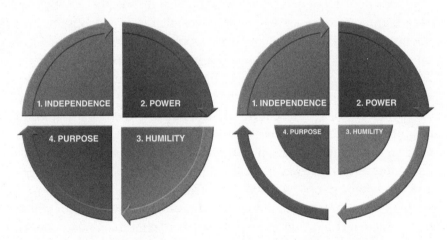

FIGURE 9.2   Balanced Circle

FIGURE 9.3   High Power and Independence-Driven Circle

If the assessment were to reveal that you have a balanced Circle:

♦ Your actions would be driven by your need to be useful elsewhere.

- The others in the meeting would perceive your actions to be reasonable, and your goal for leaving the meeting would have been to achieve some greater good elsewhere in the organization.
- You would perceive the group you left not as having been a waste of your time or theirs.
- You simply would have felt that a greater good could be achieved by all as a result of your absence.

If, on the other hand, your Circle was imbalanced and driven by independence and power:

- You would probably be perceived as being insensitive and overbearing.
- You would have left the meeting because you judged it to be a waste of your time.
- Your main goal would have been to demonstrate your power rather than to serve a greater good.

Often your action itself is less of an issue than the driver of your action. Many people have trained themselves to outwardly reflect prosocial behaviors so that others perceive them to be positive, powerful, or sincere. Yet, they are out of balance and their imbalance shows up in ways that are far less than optimal for themselves and for others.

The assessment or deep self-reflection on the issues as you go through the book gets to the core of the latent drivers of your behavior and can you help unlock your potential as your personal awareness of those drivers is increased.

Example 2: Power and Purpose–Driven with Low Independence and Humility

On Ash Wednesday, an executive (who proclaims herself to be a Christian) ensures that she stops at church *prior to arriving at work* so that she spends the entire day showing everyone the ashes on her forehead.

Her Circle Blueprint most likely reflects either of the following:

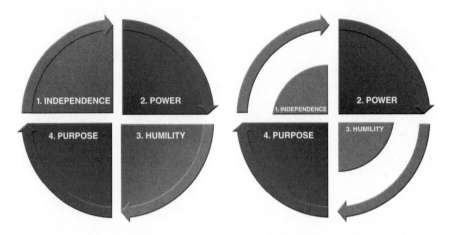

FIGURE 9.4   **Balanced Circle**   FIGURE 9.5   **High Power and Purpose-Driven Circle**

If the assessment were to reveal that she had a balanced Circle:

- ◆ Her actions would be driven by the simple desire to display her faith to all whom she encounters.
- ◆ The people she encounters throughout the day would perceive her actions to be truthful and sincere.
- ◆ She would have no judgments toward those in the organization who are not displaying ashes.
- ◆ With balanced independence she would have no concern for those with whom her religious display creates affinity or for those who might be put off by it.

If, on the other hand her Circle was imbalanced and this person was lacking independence and humility:

- ◆ This act would be driven by the need to be accepted by others (perhaps a Catholic boss).
- ◆ Her actions could be an attempt to show moral authority (low independence and humility).

◆ She would be perceived by the organization in an unflattering way, perhaps as having an overly pious or judgmental attitude.

Examples such as these can sometimes spark strong reactions. That is why we include it. You might ask yourself what is more important, the outward sign (ashes) or the inward intention? If you believe the inward intention establishes the value of the outward sign you understand why becoming clear about our intentions is so critically important. It is possible that neither she nor the people who see her truly understand the reason she is displaying the ashes. But, her true intention is having an impact, either positive or negative. It is either a display of her balance, in which case her sincerity of heart will shine, or it is a hidden effort at manipulating how she is viewed, which will ultimately lead to nowhere.

An appropriate and reliable assessment or sound self-reflection can unlock the latent drivers of your behavior. What is especially noteworthy is that often people are completely unaware of their imbalance and are acting on patterned behaviors that are creating misery in their lives and in the lives of those around them. It is important to note that we are not passing judgment. We simply see these imbalances as traps that take you off the path of thriving and reduce your chance to unlock your potential and greatness.

Example 3: High Independence and Purpose, Combined with Low Humility and Power

Bill is an artist. He sees himself as having a higher calling than most people and intends to live his life true to that calling. Hence, he spends all of his time painting. He hasn't yet sold a piece for more than a few dollars. Even though he is 30 years old, he certainly can't support himself and so he lives with his parents and has the very same bedroom he had as a child. In fact, his parents continue to provide him with most of the essentials he needs to maintain his life. He eats at their table and, when he needs transportation, drives their car.

Bill's Circle Blueprint most likely reflects either Figure 9.6 or Figure 9.7.

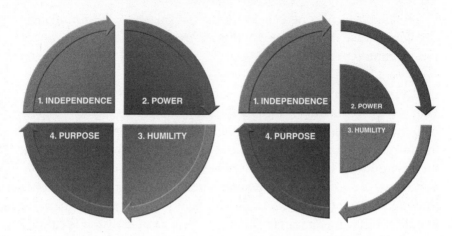

F<small>IGURE</small> 9.6   Balanced Circle

F<small>IGURE</small> 9.7   High Independence and Purpose-Driven Circle

If Bill's Circle is truly balanced:

♦ He would have accurately assessed that he has unusual talent as an artist.
♦ His commitment to his craft would be sacrificial on his part, an investment in his calling that one day would prove itself with success and notoriety.
♦ Bill would regret being a burden on his folks and would do everything within his power to minimize that burden, including getting a job to support himself.

If, on the other hand, his Circle Blueprint assessment indicated he had not yet fully cultivated his power and humility:

♦ Bill's assessment of himself as a talented artist would likely be more of a wish than a reality.
♦ He would be either unaware of his imposition on his parents or insensitive to it. It is likely he would feel entitled to their support because he believes himself to be so special.
♦ Bill may be inclined to foster the fantasy of his talent despite persistent evidence to the contrary. Rather than becoming more useful in the world around him, he could become progressively more irrelevant.

Perhaps you know someone like Bill. It may be a chronically underemployed husband who believes he deserves a much better job but won't do what it takes to obtain it. Or the dreamer who thinks she is a talented musician and dominates her church choir even though she can't carry a tune. People such as these have not yet discovered their power, and yet have somehow created a social system that enables them to live with the appearance of autonomy and independence even though they have no real independence or autonomy at all.

Parents can foster this unhealthy pattern in their children when they take on excessive responsibility for their children's welfare. It is certainly necessary for parents to provide necessities for their children including food, shelter, clothing, instruction, correction, advice, and guidance. But, when parents feel obligated to provide designer clothes, state-of-the-art electronics, the best private schools, world travel, and a college and graduate school education, the effort to prepare children for the future can backfire. Such excessive provision may actually undermine their children's independence and their successful quest to discover their unique power and place in the world. Instead of creating a solid base for success, parents can unintentionally foster their children's attachment to inflated fantasies of their giftedness and unrealistic expectations about life.

Sir Richard Branson is someone whose parents knew not to make that mistake. He tells this story of his early childhood:

> *There is a rather well-known story about Mum stopping the car on the way home from a shopping trip and telling me to find my own way home—about three miles through the countryside, and I was somewhere around five years old. She was punishing me for causing mischief in the back seat, but she was also teaching me a larger lesson about overcoming my disabling shyness and learning to ask others for directions.*
>
> *When hours had past, the sun was setting and Richard had not yet arrived home, his parents went looking for him. He had made friends with a farmer and was happily riding with him on his tractor. (Preston 2013)*

While it might seem irresponsible to leave a five-year-old child on the road alone, such challenges became opportunities for Branson to cultivate his resources. He learned to take responsibility for himself, to think creatively, to engage others when needed, and to master his fears. Many of the skills that he learned early in life equipped him well to go on to be a world adventurer and wildly successful businessman.

Because it is so natural for parents to want to provide and protect their children, they often get in the way of the critical life lessons that are necessary to gain independence, find power, learn humility, and discover purpose. Unfortunately, these parental miscalculations can leave their children with distortions in their Circles that undermine the quality and impact of their lives.

Example 4: Power and Purpose-Driven, with Low Independence and Humility

Your father-in-law has a good job and some level of financial security. He decides that it would be a great idea to take the entire family (meaning your husband/wife, kids, brothers- and sisters-in-law, etc.) on a vacation cruise during the Christmas holidays. This would require that you spend the only vacation time remaining for the year on this trip with your extended family. You're also not overly excited about spending the entire holiday with your spouse's siblings and their spouses.

Your father-in-law announces the trip and tells everyone the tickets have been ordered. Your father-in-law's Circle Blueprint most likely reflects either Figure 9.8 or 9.9.

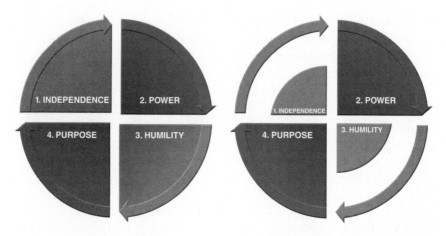

FIGURE 9.8   Balanced Circle   FIGURE 9.9   High Power and Purpose-
Driven Circle

If the assessment were to reveal that your father-in-law had a balanced Circle:

♦ His actions would be driven by his desire to provide for his family.
♦ The family would likely perceive his actions to be well intended and the gesture to be heartfelt and genuine.
♦ He would see the gesture as simply trying to be nice and do something for others he loves rather than as an exertion of his power or showing off his wealth.

If, on the other hand his Circle was imbalanced and driven by power and purpose:

♦ He may have been driven by his belief that he knows what is best for everyone regardless of what they say.
♦ He may think that you are not taking this type of vacation because you cannot afford to do so, thus he considers himself to be very giving.
♦ His main goal would be to demonstrate control and power rather than to provide a relaxing trip for the family.

The lack of independence in this imbalanced Circle expresses itself through his inability to know what makes him happy that presses him to piggyback on the fun he wants to make happen for others. The lack of humility in this profile would show up in his blindness to the true wishes of others and his insensitivity to the very idea that not everyone might want to spend their precious holiday and vacation time with dear old Dad. If he is out of balance, the result will be a vacation filled with tension, frustration, and resentment that will catch him by surprise as he fails to understand the drivers of his actions.

Example 5: Power, Humility, and Purpose-Driven, with Low Independence

This example is very common and demonstrates the importance of having mastered independence before life can flourish.

A very powerful and wealthy man has taken the day off work to hang out with some friends. He lives in an affluent neighborhood in a large home. When his friends arrive at his house the man greets them at the door wearing only his dress shirt, boxer shorts, and dress socks—no pants. He invites his visitors into the kitchen. When they arrive they find several pairs of dress shoes strewn over the counter. The man begins the conversation with his visitors as he continues shining his shoes.

The visitors finally ask the man why he is standing in his boxer shorts in his kitchen polishing his shoes? He laughs and responds that his wife is out of town. The men are puzzled. The wealthy man explains that his wife doesn't allow him to walk around the house in his boxer shorts and he is not allowed to shine his shoes in the kitchen.

The wealthy man's Circle Blueprint most likely reflects either of the following:

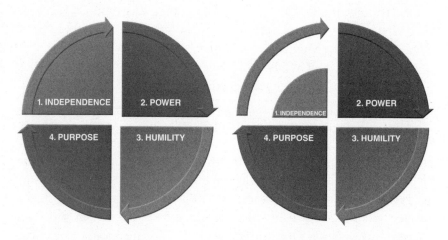

FIGURE 9.10   Balanced Circle   FIGURE 9.11   **High Power, Humility, and Purpose-Driven Circle**

If the assessment were to reveal the wealthy man had a balanced Circle:

- His actions would be driven by his desire to engage in actions that are not pleasing to his wife but in a respectful way. He waits until she's out of town so he can relax, but there is no sense of having an "I'll show her who's boss" attitude.

If, on the other hand his Circle was imbalanced and driven by his lack of independence:

- ◆ He may have been driven by his desire to engage in any behavior displeasing to his wife while she's away.
- ◆ His main goal would have been to demonstrate that he can and will do whatever he wants, even if he has to do it behind her back. He feels a sense of control while she's away.

The good news is that you can get on track and make progress toward your goals by balancing your Circle. It doesn't matter where or when you start in balancing your Circle in order to find true fulfillment. What is important is that you start on the life-changing process that can advance you from a life of mere survival to a rich life in which you can thrive and prosper.

The Assessment Process

- ◆ You will begin by assessing your activities; what's in your Circle? This will help you see how you spend your time and how you feel about the choices you've made as you've prioritized your life.
- ◆ As you work your way through each chapter, you will better understand each key element of your Circle Blueprint. At the end of each chapter you will be invited to complete the core assessment for that element or to reflect on this issue yourself. The assessment we provide will show you the results as you complete each chapter and compare the results with the preassessment. We will provide you with your detailed Circle Blueprint assessment. You may wish to do this through self-reflection instead. Either way, you will have clarity about the areas where you need better balance and the specific factors of each element where you need the most work. This map will guide your development.

The immediate feedback assessment methodology enables you to gain insight into your growth through the interaction with the concepts that we presented. As you experience the power of growing and developing awareness, you will learn that you have the power to make real and constructive change in your life. This power emancipates you from whatever has been diminishing your spirit. As you balance and expand your Circle you will see that you have within you everything you need to thrive.

To begin your assessment process, please go to www.thecircle blueprint.com to create your logon. Your assessment is confidential. You will be the only one who sees your results. Once you log in you will be invited to begin the assessment. Alternately, if you are not interested in the actual assessment, substitute honest self-reflection as we go.

Chapter 10

Independence

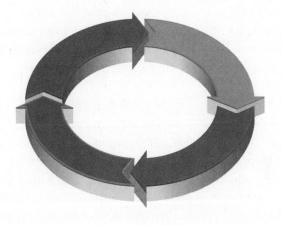

The Journey

Each of us is on a journey; the journey of your life. We pass through life poorly, wonderfully, or somewhere between. We may be fully aware of our choices along the way and wise in how we make them or we might be unconscious and quite unaware of both what we are creating and what we are missing. The one thing that is true for each of us is that the journey is a one-way street. You can't go back and you don't get to start over.

One of the great dangers in the journey of life is to blindly follow the rules we were given as children. There is nothing wrong with the rules themselves but there comes a time when you must think for yourself.

Most of us were taught to be good people and to be responsible; both wonderful traits. But, it may be possible to be so focused on being good and responsible that we miss out on our lives; the ones that belong to us. We may hope to be rewarded someday for our obedience only to discover that day never comes.

If so, we failed to discover our independence.

The Independence Element

Independence is the first and most fundamental step in achieving the maturity and satisfaction of a rich and balanced life Circle. Being independent means casting off all forms of dependence to gain the freedom to live your life—the unique life that belongs to you—in an unrestricted and unencumbered manner. It is our starting place because it is the most challenging and most fundamental step you can take. Until independence is mastered, development in the other three areas cannot occur. Without independence, you will not have a balanced life.

Independence is about taking 100 percent responsibility for your life and the outcomes of your choices. Independence is living with freedom from the self-talk and the torment of inner doubts and inse-curities. Independence is the ability to be undistracted by anxiety over the future and by guilt about the past such that you are fully aware of the power present in each moment. Independence is free-dom from the drama created by others and from the stories in your head that create drama in your life. Those who have mastered inde-pendence understand that they are the source of all their success and of all their limitations. They don't perceive themselves to be at the mercy of anyone or anything. They never blame or complain. They only ask the questions, "How did I create this outcome?" And "What do I want to create now?"

Six factors influence your ability to gain independence. They are:

1. Decreasing *crisis-prone* behavior. People who are crisis-prone need to surround themselves with chaos, crises, and prob-lems whether they actually exist or not. We call this drama. Drama can be defined as manufacturing emotional distress when it is not justified. We create drama by the stories we make up about life. We can create stories about how things aren't fair that make us feel scared so we act like victims. We can make up stories about how bad or wrong people are that make us angry. Those stories make us villains. Or, we can create stories about how much people need us to rescue them that cause us to act like heroes. Those who are not crisis-prone certainly don't manufacture emotional distress. Instead, they are steady in how they live their lives, focused on moving forward and not easily distracted. They face issues squarely and with the purpose of resolving them as best they can.

Crisis-prone behavior creates confusion, disruption, and upset that are often unnecessary. We all know people who seem to be in constant strife—they tell us about the huge tragedies in their lives—every flat tire or minor argument seems to involve a story more complex than most Hollywood movies. They seem to generate crisis and star in their own dramatic story. Their constant state of upset distracts them from the need to deal with reality and the issues that stand in their way.

2. Increasing levels of *autonomy*. People with low autonomy see themselves as needy. They may view themselves as victims of their background or circumstances. They see others as better equipped to deal with life and have an expectation that others should take care of them or help them out. They constantly compare themselves and assess inferiority and superiority of self and others. Those with high autonomy like the feeling of taking care of themselves. They focus on continuously developing new skills, solving whatever problems arise, and doing as much for themselves as possible—not comparing themselves to others, but rather, appreciating everyone's uniqueness.

Another friend of ours claimed that he hardly ever compared himself to others. He was quite happy with his life and with himself. But, after speaking with us about comparison, he began to see things differently.

I didn't think I compared myself at all. But, it is almost as if once my eyes were open to this idea, I saw myself measuring myself against others almost everywhere. I was in a business meeting this morning, and the guy I was meeting with had on a shirt that was very neatly starched. Mine was wrinkled and, suddenly, I felt self-conscious and somehow weaker than I had a few moments before. I really like my new car, but when I pulled up at a light and next to me was the new Mercedes AMG-GT, my car seemed a bit shabby. I was at the gym and couldn't help but notice that I was lifting more weight than the guys working out next to me. I hate to admit it, but I got a good feeling. I like the idea of being stronger than they are. I imagine I work harder at staying in shape than they do. They are probably lazier than am I. And this was just my morning.

What is wrong with comparing yourself to others? Who doesn't want to keep up with the Joneses? Whether it is how many friends we have on Facebook, the size of our home, our weed-free green lawn, the amount we spend on our clothes or our education, we are often noticing who has more and who has less than we do.

Our friend didn't think he had an issue with comparing. But, he wasn't aware. He was so used to comparing himself to others that it seemed natural; it was normal. It was only when he began to look for it that he saw how pervasive and frequent this behavior was.

3. Reducing your need to succeed by *pleasing others*. People who have a high orientation toward pleasing others cultivate the ability to adapt to the social demands of those around them. They take their cues as to what they should say and how they should react from whoever appears to have the resources they need. In grade school these people would have been called the "teacher's pet." As adults they are often insincere, pretending to be supportive even when they are truly resentful and envious. People with a low orientation to please others are more interested in knowing and speaking their own minds. This is not to say that they are rude or brash, but rather, they are authentic and sincere. They are likely to have the ability to read others and fit in, but they won't compromise themselves to do so.

One man shared a painful story about misdirected pleasing:

I married at a very young age and my wife was younger than me. I thought the way to create a successful marriage was to please and that is exactly what I set out to do. I helped my wife write her papers for school. I worked so she didn't have to. I paid the bills, took on many of the tasks of running the household and, as time passed, shared a great deal of the child-rearing. I didn't mind doing any of these things. I wanted her to be happy.

Yet, the oddest thing occurred. Instead of being happy, my wife seemed to become progressively more unhappy, even angry. She seemed to increasingly resent me. It was quite perplexing to me. We went on this way for more than 20 years. I worked harder and harder to win her happiness while feeling my marriage was slipping away.

One night, I was done. I simply couldn't do it anymore. It was too hard. I stopped pleasing. Those were dark days. I moved out of the bedroom and into the basement. I knew what was coming. Soon I was asked to leave my home. I packed up my few things and drove away from my home, my children, my wife, and the life I had built. I sacrificed my friends and my reputation.

But I also felt an odd sense of something positive stirring as if I had found some lost part of myself. Despite the pain of it all, I felt the stirring of a freedom that seemed powerful.

Our friend thought he was on the right path by doing whatever he could to please his wife. He knew his parents' marriage had not been very happy. Surely, he would do better. Creating a wonderful relationship simply required being better than his dad and mom had been at pleasing each other. He gave himself to this task with passion and commitment. How surprising it was to him when he discovered that, in the end, pleasing didn't work. Pleasing could not create the marriage he hoped for. Quite the opposite; pleasing eroded whatever good had been in his relationship. The more he worked at pleasing, the more he lost himself in the process. Rather than thriving, he sensed his life was eroding. Failing to understand the need to find his voice and to bring himself to the marriage, he took his emptiness as a signal to try even harder to please his wife.

We have discovered this to be universally true. Pleasing leads, at best, to mediocrity. You may think that by becoming who your boss wants you to be you will be promoted to the corner office. What you may not see is that while you are trying to become the person your boss wants you to be, you are not cultivating your unique gifts and abilities that would have been your true source of power and the basis of your continued success. When you are fitting into the expectations of your friends, you are minimizing your unique character and interests—the things that truly make you special and desirable. Whether we are pretending to be what our friends, our family, our boss, or the world wants us to be, we are setting ourselves up for being less than who we were designed to be.

4. Increasing your individualism by reducing your *pretentiousness*. Those who are high on this scale have a need to appear more accomplished and successful than they are. How they look is very important. They want to come across in a way that puts them in the most favorable light. Those who are low in pretentiousness are focused more on their accomplishments than on how they are seen. They want to do things that matter. They don't feel much of a need for their accomplishments to be recognized.

One of the greatest figures in history who demonstrated the power of unpretentiousness was Jesus of Nazareth. He was born in an obscure town in the middle of nowhere. He was raised by a carpenter who taught him that trade. He was an untrained rabbi who traveled on foot from town to town to declare the good news of the Kingdom of God. Those who embraced pretentiousness opposed him. They were the religious leaders. They dressed in fine clothes. They imposed religious law on others. They reveled in their power and influence. At first, they ignored Jesus. He was a nobody. Nothing would come of him.

But, he had a power they lacked. He spoke with authority. He healed the sick. He fed the masses. He was the real deal and the world recognized him as such. Then the religious leaders were threatened by him. Even though outwardly he was a nobody, inwardly it was undeniable that he was a somebody. He was more popular than they were. He was more powerful than they were. He had something they didn't have.

They had but one recourse: kill him. So, they masterminded his death. This would be the end, they thought. Kill him and it will be over. They would be in charge again. But their pretentiousness made them shortsighted, as it always does.

While they were able to have him killed, they were not able to defeat him. His life was bigger than their pretense. His influence only expanded. Now his message is spread throughout the world. What a story!

5. Decreasing *reliance* from being controlled by someone or something else. People who are high in reliance depend on the support and favor of others. They often attach themselves to people and institutions that offer security and avoid places and people that insist on meritocracy. Those who are self-reliant have no expectation of gaining recognition or reward for anything they did not accomplish. They expect to be treated fairly and are uncomfortable if they are given more than they believe they deserve. Reliance on drugs or alcohol, overindulgence in television as a means to zone out, going numb through all time-wasting behaviors—these choices rob you of the experience of your life. Becoming aware of these dependences and choosing alternatives that put you in ever-increasing awareness of your life experience are critical to having a rich and full Circle.

Everyone is reliant to some degree. For example, each of us would scarcely exist as the only person on Earth and we all need food to stay alive. We all likely understand that overreliance on harmful drugs will create problems, too. But we can be reliant in ways that are not as obvious as drug dependency and seem more innocent yet, just like drugs, exert control on our lives. Each of us needs to take time to relax and unwind. But sometimes the choices we make as to how to relax such as drinking to take the edge off, can numb our ability to fully enjoy the richness of our lives.

I work hard every day. My days start early and I am in the office by 6:30 A.M. I have a cup of coffee at home, stop at Starbucks along my way into work, and need another cup when I am at my desk.

The caffeine gives me an edge; I can feel my motor racing. Now I am ready to go. Normally, my mornings are filled with meetings. There is a lot going on so I often check my e-mail during the meetings and sometimes step out to take a call. I have been told that multitasking isn't the best use of my time, but frankly, I have so much on my plate that it is necessary. Lunch? Oh, I usually eat it at my desk. I can't really remember what was on that sandwich I had today. Of course I was reading e-mail when I was eating. I usually get home around 7 P.M. We have dinner together as a family and usually in front of the TV. This is the only time I can catch up on the news. Yeah, I have a drink with dinner and then a few after the kids are in bed. They help me unwind so I can get to sleep. Sometimes when the stress is bad, I need medication to get to sleep. But not often. It is normal to live this way, right? I mean … I am successful.

Our friend is a normal, busy, and successful man. And, his life is pretty heavily dependent on a variety of crutches that he views as aids to his success. He probably isn't sleeping well because he is drinking too much alcohol. He makes up for the lack of sleep with caffeine. Rather than giving all of his attention to that which is immediately before him, he does two or three things at the same time, thinking he is being efficient while sacrificing his creativity. He isn't enjoying his coffee or his time with his family or his drink after work as much as he could be because they are all tools he is using to manage his life. He is reliant in many ways that might seem innocent enough, but end up controlling him. Many of us make similar choices every day. We become numb to life in small ways—not obvious ones—and may not see the full impact of our choices.

6. Having *personal commitment* means having goals, operationalizing them into actionable plans, and disciplining yourself to execute those plans. Those low in personal commitment make pledges to accomplish certain tasks and often lack the discipline or desire to succeed. Those high in personal commitment make clear their obligations and reliably keep them. The absence of personal commitment is a sign of immaturity, signifying that you have made very few things in life important to you and/or that you have little sense of

responsibility for the world around you. Life is easy if we limit our commitments. We can come and go as we please. There is no one counting on us. But achievement requires the discipline of personal commitment. You can't succeed in much unless you commit to it to the best of your ability.

If you have been to a small town, you likely know the setting—everyone knows everyone. One client who grew up in such a small town recounted a story of going to the hardware store with his grandfather as young boy. Walking into the store he saw a man he knew to be very poor across the street. Minutes later the man came into the hardware store and gave his grandfather five dollars. When they got in the truck his grandfather said, "son, I want you to remember this. I haven't had my grocery shop in 20 years, but that man still tries to pay off the grocery credit he ran up."

Not too many years ago, the personal commitment embodied by a poor man still trying to make good on his word to pay for groceries was well understood. There was modest need for lawyers and contracts because when people gave their word, they created a bond and made a commitment that they would keep.

Our words of commitment create our lives far more than we might recognize. When we make commitments that we don't keep, people come to see us as unreliable. Their trust in us diminishes. The value they place in us is reduced.

On the other hand, when we keep our word, we demonstrate strong personal commitment. People know we can be relied upon. We become trustworthy, worthy of the trust of others. Hence, we become more useful to those around us and our opportunities expand.

Independence Chapter Summary

It is possible to have all the appearances of a successful life: financial wealth, advanced degrees, career success, a long and happy marriage and yet still feel trapped, powerless, and unhappy if you haven't mastered independence. If you bypass independence, your power will not fulfill its potential because it will always be filtered through the need to please others. Your ability to effectively use all of the elements of the Circle—power, humility, and purpose—are limited by the degree to which you are able to master independence.

Each of the six factors can increase your independence through:

1. Recognizing your reaction to the problems, obstacles, and crises that arise. While you may feel a rising sense of panic, take a deep breath, wait for your anxiety to subside, reflect on your options, pick the best one, and move forward. Resist the temptation to act without thinking, which may only make matters worse.

2. Taking 100 percent responsibility for all of your decisions and their outcomes. Such radical ownership of your life choices puts you in the strongest position to learn from your successes and mistakes and to make course corrections that will make you even more effective.

3. Listening to your own thoughts, opinions, preferences, and desires and believing in the power of your uniqueness to create your success rather than trying to succeed by pretending to be what others want you to be and conforming to their wishes.

4. Being careful to be completely honest in how you represent yourself wherever you go, not taking credit you don't deserve, not pretending to be who you are not, and not concealing who you truly are. Your acceptance of the truth about yourself betrays a powerful confidence.

5. Shedding all reliance on people and things that trap you in dependency or numb your ability to be fully alive and demonstrating deep and open appreciation for those who make a healthy and meaningful contribution to your life.

6. Being careful about the commitments you make because you take giving your word seriously. Following through on every commitment because you know your character is built on your reliability.

Each of the same six factors can also decrease your independence in the following ways:

1. Reacting to every problem you face as if it is a crisis and choosing to live in constant emotional turmoil will cloud your thinking and make it difficult to make effective decisions.

2. Avoiding personal responsibility by fostering dependency on others will undermine your ability to grow and learn. Rather than becoming more independent, you will sacrifice the skills and abilities necessary to care for your life.

3. Seeking to please others by pretending will make it more difficult for you to discern your own thoughts and preferences and will conceal from you and others your true strengths and gifts.

4. Pretending to be what you are not undermines your confidence in yourself and leads to a life of deception. The longer this pattern continues, the more difficult it is to rediscover the truth about yourself.

5. Overreliance on the wrong things will foster dependence and the gradual erosion of your awareness of your strength and aliveness.

6. Not committing to things or committing and not following through undermines your integrity and leads to mistrust. You will mistrust your own ability to do what is best for yourself, and others will find you unreliable.

Note: Please feel free to tear out this page for reference as you work through this chapter.

Independence

Independence is about taking 100 percent responsibility for your life and the outcomes of your choices. Independence is living with freedom from the self-talk and the torment of inner doubts and insecurities. Independence is the ability to be undistracted by anxiety over the future and by guilt about the past, such that you are fully present to the power present in each moment. Independence is freedom from the drama created by others and from the stories in your head that create drama in your life. Those who have mastered independence understand that they are the source of all of their success and of all of their limitations. They don't perceive themselves to be at the mercy of anyone or anything. They never blame or complain. They only ask the questions, "How did I create this outcome?" And "What do I want to create now?"

- ♦ Crisis-Prone Behaviors
  People who are crisis-prone tend to fill their lives with drama. They prefer to be emotionally upset.
- ♦ Autonomous
  People with low autonomy see themselves as lacking in personal freedom and may be needy.
- ♦ Pleasing
  People who have a high orientation toward pleasing others cultivate the ability to adapt to the social demands of those around them.
- ♦ Pretentious
  Those who are high on this scale have a need to appear more accomplished and successful than they are. How they look is very important.
- ♦ Reliance
  People who are high in reliance depend on the support and favor of others.
- ♦ Personal Commitment
  Those who are low in personal commitment either don't make commitments or don't follow through on the ones they make. They are unreliable.

ACTION STEP ONE

Return to www.thecircleblueprint.com to complete the full assessment for independence. Review the results before progressing to Chapter 11: Power. Alternately, if you are not interested in the actual assessment, take time for honest self-reflection on each element.

ACTION STEP TWO

After you take the assessment, move on to the exercises that follow. We offer exercises for each factor. In areas where you are not thriving, there is room for growth. If you want additional exercises, please consider our series of workbooks, available online at www.thecircle blueprint.com.

Steps to Reduce Crisis-Prone Behaviors

1. Pay attention to what you are doing and saying. Recognize when you are creating drama.
2. Don't become a part of other people's drama. Don't allow yourself to get sucked in.
3. Rethink your relationships. Reduce your contact with people who are caught in drama.
4. Be a straight shooter. Be clear, honest, and graceful in your communication with all people.
5. Know the difference between conflict that is critical to fulfilling your destiny and that which is not. Engage only in conflict that holds the possibility of positive change.

Steps to Increase Autonomy

1. Notice how often you wait to make a decision until you have canvassed the opinions of others and assessed their anticipated reaction.
2. Notice how often you hold back on doing something you want because you fear criticism or judgment from others.
3. Notice how often you copy others in order to fit in.
4. Practice noticing your unique thoughts, values, feelings, and desires.

5. Practice expressing yourself more fully.

6. Become aware of the feeling of freedom and power that comes from expanding your self-expression.

Steps to Reduce Pleasing Behaviors

1. Notice when you are pretending to be what someone else wants you to be rather than being yourself.

2. Notice when you are not telling the truth or saying what you really think.

3. Practice expressing your thoughts and desires even in small things like the movie you want to see or what you want to eat for lunch.

4. Practice saying no when you don't want to do something someone else wants to do.

5. Notice when you feel trapped or unhappy in a relationship and take this as a sign that you might be making pleasing more important than being yourself.

6. Practice expressing yourself more openly, sharing your ideas, thoughts, plans, and dreams.

Steps to Reduce Pretentiousness

1. Notice when you are taking credit for something you didn't do, or when you are boasting over something you did and are acting as if you are more important than you are.

2. Notice when you buy things only to show them off to others.

3. See if you can identify your insecurity about not being good enough that drives you to show off and boast. Write it down.

4. Practice accepting yourself in whatever area you feel insecure or inadequate.

5. Practice sharing your weaknesses, fears, and insecurities with others.

Steps to Reduce Reliance

1. Make a list of all of the things you could do for yourself that you are depending on someone else to do.
2. Make a plan to take ownership of everything on your previous list.
3. Start putting your plans into action.
4. List everything you do that wastes time (for example, watching television) and/or dulls your awareness (for example, drinking alcohol).
5. Decide how you would alter these behaviors to support greater awareness.
6. Start putting your plans into action.

Steps to Increase Personal Commitments

1. Make a list of goals you have for yourself but have not achieved. How many have you not even started making progress toward?
2. Make a list of promises you have made to others that you have not kept. List some of the consequences to those relationships that have resulted.
3. Be careful about what you commit to do. Commit only to things you want to complete.
4. Be clear in your commitments as to exactly what you are committing to do and by when.
5. Keep a list of all of your commitments.
6. Take responsibility, apologize, and make amends for commitments you fail to keep.

Chapter 11

Power

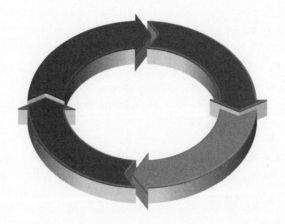

M any people view themselves as quite ordinary; as if there is nothing all that special about them. There is certainly a great deal of truth in that judgment. There are so many ways we are like each other; so much we have in common.

What you may fail to know about yourself is that you also possess something quite extraordinary. Some people are lucky enough to discover their gift early in life and so live in its power for much of their lives. Others never discover that uniqueness and so live their lives without ever experiencing that sense of being truly special.

It is your extraordinary self that is meant to be the source of power to live your life. It is meant to supply you with material success, purpose and meaning, and a sense of security that you have something to offer that the world needs.

The second step in cultivating a truly meaningful life is cultivating real power. Power can come from many sources. But the power to which we refer is that which comes from discovering your unique giftedness and in fully aligning your energy and passion with it. Your work in life was not meant to be drudgery that you endure because you need to pay the bills. Your work was meant to be the creative expression of your true gifts. When you understand your gifts and work from that place, your work becomes a source of power that provides for your needs but also impacts the world in amazing ways.

It is this power we encourage you to seek.

In 2005, Steve Jobs addressed the graduating class at Stanford University. He told three stories. The first was of his adoption as an infant. The second was of starting Apple in his parents' garage when he was 20 years old. The third story was of being diagnosed with pancreatic cancer and told he was going to die. He viewed each of these as pivotal stories in his life. Then he gave this advice to his audience:

> *No one wants to die. Even people who want to go to heaven don't want to die to get there. And yet death is the destination we all share. No one has ever escaped it. And that is as it should be, because Death is very likely the single best invention of Life. It is Life's change agent. It clears out the old to make way for the new. Right now the new is you, but someday not too long from now, you will gradually become the old and be cleared away. Sorry to be so dramatic, but it is quite true.*
>
> *Your time is limited, so don't waste it living someone else's life. Don't be trapped by dogma—which is living with the results of other people's thinking. Don't let the noise of others' opinions drown out your own inner voice. And most important, have the courage to follow your heart and intuition. They somehow already know what you truly want to become. Everything else is secondary.*
>
> —Steve Jobs

Jobs was encouraging all those present to find their power, the thing they were meant to do in life. He believed this to be the most important lesson he had learned from life and this advice to be his greatest gift to those young people who were entering their professional lives.

The Power Element

Your power was with you when you were small, the result of your unique genetics and the influence of those who raised you. From time to time, it became clear to the people who cared about you that you were special in some way. Perhaps a teacher noticed you were a natural leader or a coach pointed out that your ability to throw a baseball stood out. Hopefully, your giftedness became so clear to you that you saw its value, embraced it as your treasure, and began purposefully cultivating and developing it. That child who wildly danced in the rain took tap, jazz, and ballet lessons and just knew she had something special. This seed of dance was carefully tended until it blossomed within a talented ballerina.

But not everyone was this lucky. Not everyone had people watching so carefully and reflecting that which they saw. Not everyone came to know what was so special about her life. And, because she never saw it, that uniqueness was not developed. Instead of living in the passion of her creative ability, her true power, her work is only the means to the end of providing the money she needs for her life.

It is never too late to find your power—it never goes away. Right now it might be showing up in your hobbies and interests; even though you are working as a lawyer, you have the most beautiful and abundant vegetable garden that any farmer would envy. It takes courage to discover and then invest in your power, and it isn't easy to realize later in life that you have been headed in the wrong direction. But the sooner you have that realization, the more quickly you can get lined up with your power—the power you need to live an exceptional life.

There are six factors that comprise the power element.

1. *Self-determination* means to establish your own goals and to move steadily toward them regardless of distraction or difficulty. Those who are high in self-determination are not

only clear as to where they are headed, they also know why they are headed there. They possess the ability to discipline themselves to finish what they start. Those who are low in self-determination either don't set goals or take on goals that might be meaningful to others, but aren't to them. They might be fulfilling their parents' wishes or trying to avoid conflict by going along with their friends' wishes. They often take the path of least resistance that, ironically, often creates more difficulty for them in the end.

How many people actually heed Jobs's sage advice to "have the courage to follow your heart and intuition" and use it to guide their lives? Far too often the story goes something like this:

My job is really boring. It was boring when I took the job and it has been boring ever since. I am doing the same old thing over and over again. I haven't learned anything new in years. I have no idea where our company is headed, if it is headed anywhere. I really don't care what they say when the leaders have those meetings to talk about vision. It always sounds like the flavor of the month. Not only don't I like my job, I don't like the people I work for. It seems to me that they are getting rich on my back. What can I do? It's a job. It isn't supposed to be fun. That's why they call it work!

We hope this isn't your story. It certainly doesn't have to be. Your work was meant to be an expression of your creativity, the opportunity for you to do what you love every day. It is here that you will find your greatest success. If your gift is to make shoes, you can become an amazing shoemaker. If it is to teach, you can be an outstanding teacher. Every day will be an opportunity for you to hone your craft, to cultivate your skill, and to indulge your natural interest. You will be living in your power.

2. *Self-efficacy* refers to your belief in yourself. Those who are high in self-efficacy believe they are capable of success in many areas—they know that if they put their mind to something, they can achieve a certain level of mastery

at it. In contrast, those low in self-efficacy often do not attempt new challenges because they lack confidence that they will succeed. Self-efficacy is often explained by the "self-determined prophecy" or the aphorism that whether you think you can or you think you can't, you're right! It is the belief in self, or lack thereof, that often determines whether a person is actually successful at even the simplest task.

> *Not everyone could see my gift. My high school coach cut me from my high school team. But, looking back I can see that it was one of the best things that happened to me. I was cocky, so full of myself that I couldn't see clearly how blessed I was to have this skill. I got over myself and applied myself even more to the game of basketball. Many people told me that I was wasting my time. They kept saying that no one could make a living playing basketball. I didn't care what they said. I loved the game!*
>
> *Now, I am playing in the NBA. My career is doing what I enjoy. And I am a star! Who would have imagined that I could have done so well from applying myself to playing a game? Wow!*

Do you recognize this man as Michael Jordan? He believed in himself and kept working—eventually realizing his dream. He certainly had the talent and could have been discouraged by being cut but he was not deterred; he knew he could succeed. It is this kind of confidence in yourself that you need to cultivate if you are to live in your power.

3. *Achievement-striving*. This trait speaks to your ability to harness your energy and skills in a manner that can produce positive results. Those who have developed this skill are able to maximize their productivity. They use their time and resources judiciously and minimize wasted time and effort. Those who are low in this skill find themselves wishing for things to occur, procrastinating and wasting time. They have

difficulty getting their act together sufficiently to make things happen and pursue actions with a lack of direction, focus, and passion.

Almost every successful person, regardless of how you define success, understands the importance of striving. Very few things in life worth having are gained without effort. The greater your ambition, the more difficult the challenges you will face whether you are a writer, a musician, or a mother.

> *Kobe's professional trainer was fast asleep. Could you blame him? It was 3:30* AM *in the morning. All a sudden his phone starts ringing. It's Kobe. He must be in trouble, or in some kind of emergency. His trainer is freaking out, and nervously picks up the phone.*
>
> *Kobe says that he's doing some conditioning work and could use his trainer's help. The trainer then proceeds to get ready and head over to the gym. He arrives around 4:30* AM. *What did he see? He saw Kobe by himself practicing. Drenched in sweat, it looked like he just jumped in a pool. It wasn't even 5* AM *in the morning yet."*
>
> —AJ Agrawal

Success takes hard work. It requires focus, determination, and self-sacrifice. It is not costly to want a better life but it is to build one. Everyone needs to look in the mirror and ask himself, "How hard am I willing to try to get where I want to go?"

4. *Zest* points to the energy you bring to life. Those who are high in zest exude enthusiasm in all their pursuits. They are "gas pedals" for the world around them, advancing their plans and getting things done with vigor. They are lively and display energy in all they do—some call this having a bounce in their step. Often, those high in zest seem delighted, sparked creatively, and living a life of passion. Those who are low on this scale manifest a lethargy that is difficult for them to overcome. They seem to go through the motions and lack energy; they may be stuck in a rut or appear sluggish, and everything seems as if it is too hard or requires more resources than they have available.

There are many examples of zest, but one that stands out strikingly is from the children's book *Winnie-the-Pooh*. Contrast Tigger, who bounced around happily, with Eeyore, who moped about everywhere he went, and you'll see a clear difference in the zest with which the two characters went about their lives. We all know a Tigger or an Eeyore. It seems clear which one has zest and which one does not.

5. *Acceptance.* Contrast the words *willingly* and *reluctantly* and you will have a good understanding of acceptance. Those who are high in acceptance are open to life as it comes to them. They understand that the world is constantly changing and, if they are going to stay relevant, they need to be changing as well. Hence, they welcome new opportunities, adventures, challenges, and circumstances as opportunities to learn new things, to grow, to expand. They invite feedback, regardless of how it is given or how critical it is because they hope to see themselves as they are seen by others and to identify blind spots that limit their effectiveness.

   Those who are low in acceptance resist almost everything new and different. Change feels threatening and so is avoided. They are far more interested in maintaining the status quo than in looking for the next new opportunity. Seeing their limitations can be especially threatening, so they rarely ask for feedback and can become very defensive and angry if challenged or criticized. Resisting the natural change of life makes it difficult for people who are not accepting to keep up with the challenges of life.

Far too many brave servicemen and -women have come home from war with some devastating disability that has changed their life forever. After their wounds heal, they face the challenge of acceptance. Can they let go of the way they thought about how things would be and step into new expectation, challenges, dreams, and hopes? Such acceptance demands tremendous courage. It must not be easy. But, with acceptance come new openings. Their life has not ended, but it has changed in very big ways. Without acceptance, there is no moving forward. All that is ahead is a life of anger and pain.

We hope that none of you will have to face so profound and sacrificial a challenge. But, in much smaller (and easier) ways, life calls you to the same issue. As you age, you lose some of the ability you had in your youth. You lose a loved one and must move on without the person you cherished. You get sick or hurt and must adapt. Acceptance is the quality that allows you to flex with life and move forward. It is such a wonderful skill to possess.

6. *Self-discipline.* Those high in self-discipline are able to do the things that need to be done. They can regulate their behavior, that is, they can do things that are not always enjoyable or that are hard but that must be done in order to reach their goal. John F. Kennedy gave a speech that spoke to this ability, saying that we choose to do difficult things "not because they are easy, but because they are hard; because that goal will serve to organize and measure the best of our energies and skills, because that challenge is one that we are willing to accept, one we are unwilling to postpone." Those without self-discipline are not able to take on challenges that are difficult. Instead, they take the easy road, the one that steps around difficulty and avoids effort. But in so doing, it misses the development of character.

Self-discipline has two parts. The first is the ability to make yourself do what you might not like and isn't necessarily easy, but is absolutely necessary to get you where you want to go. It requires an assortment of tools including the ability to encourage yourself, push yourself, hold yourself accountable, reward yourself, and even punish yourself when necessary. The second is the ability to deny yourself things you want but would get in the way of what you are trying to accomplish.

Everyone has wrestled with self-discipline many times. You are determined to lose 20 lbs. and the process for doing so is pretty simple. You need to eat more of the right stuff, eat less of the bad stuff, and exercise on a regular basis. Now, comes the hard part. You must get yourself to do it! It isn't good enough to eat more of the good stuff while not eating any less of the bad stuff. It won't help much to exercise unless you have your diet under control. Practicing self-discipline every day in small things makes it easier to apply it to bigger projects.

Power Chapter Summary

Power is a very important, but often overlooked, topic. Until you have found your power, you do not know the source of your uniqueness, the thing that truly makes you special. You have not discovered the gift that makes work fun, interesting, and deeply satisfying. You may have glimpses of your power from time to time. It might show up in your hobbies. But until you have made it the center of your life, you are missing out on a great adventure and a wild ride.

Each of the six factors can increase your power through:

1. Having self-determination that manifests in taking charge of all aspects of your life and leaving nothing to chance or under the control of someone else.
2. Demonstrating strong self-efficacy in the high level of confidence you have in your ability to not only get where you want to go but also in overcoming every challenge you face along the way.
3. Showing achievement-striving in the ambitious goals you set for yourself and the amount of effort you are willing to expend to achieve them.
4. Filling yourself with zest that radiates to everyone in your enthusiasm, vigor, vitality, and optimism.
5. Accepting your life as it comes to you, the good and the bad, the easy and the difficult, the happy and the sad, with openness and grace and seeking to learn from every circumstance in order to make yourself even more effective.
6. Mastering self-discipline so you can reliably follow through on your intentions and avoid temptations that could distract you from your path.

Each of the same six factors also can decrease your power in the following ways:

1. Until you have mastered independence it will be impossible for you to put your unique power to full use. You are likely to avoid seeing it clearly or be unwilling to fully embrace it because you are not sufficiently self-determined.

2. If you are low in self-efficacy, it will be difficult to believe that you have the power to make positive changes in your life. Hence, you will easily succumb to just getting by and accepting mediocrity.

3. Without sufficient achievement-striving you are likely to set goals too low to be worthy of your greatness or to lack the willingness to work as hard as is necessary to achieve them.

4. Lower levels of zest, enthusiasm, vigor, and vitality mean decreased life energy. Your enthusiasm and vitality are the gas in your tank. If these are low, there is not sufficient energy in your life to make the changes necessary to shift to your power.

5. Lack of acceptance means you find yourself constantly fighting against whatever is occurring. You have set yourself up to resist the opportunities and challenges that must be embraced for you to have your power.

6. If you lack self-discipline if will be difficult or impossible to stick with the course you have set for yourself. You will become easily distracted by whatever issues pop up in your day and will lack the will and determination to consistently move toward your best self.

Note: Please feel free to tear out this page for reference as you work through this chapter.

Power

We define the power component as finding your unique power. We believe that every person has power in them. Some of us have found that which makes us powerful and brilliant at a young age. Others know what our power is and have not yet had the courage to follow through on that path. Still others don't yet have a clue as to that which makes them truly unique and special. It is our hope that each of you moves further down the road of discovering your power and making it the very center of your lives.

+ Self-Determination
  The commitment to take full ownership of directing your life and not allowing your life to be controlled by anyone or anything else.
+ Self-Efficacy
  The confidence to believe you can exert control over your motivation, behavior, and social environment.
+ Achievement-Striving
  The ability to set appropriately ambitious goals for yourself and the willingness to do what it takes to achieve them.
+ Zest
  This combination of traits—zest, enthusiasm, vigor, and vitality—point to the energy you bring to life.
+ Acceptance
  The openness to welcome whatever life brings and to invite and welcome feedback in order to increase your effectiveness.
+ Self-Discipline
  The ability to keep yourself on track in moving toward your goals and to avoid temptations and distractions that might derail you.

ACTION STEP ONE

Now that you have completed the chapter on power, please return to www.thecircleblueprint.com to complete the assessment. Once you complete it, you will receive the results to review before progressing to Chapter 12: Humility. Alternately, if you choose not to take the assessment, substitute honest self-reflection on each element.

ACTION STEP TWO

After you take the assessment, move on to the exercises that follow. We offer exercises for each factor. In areas where you are not thriving, there is room for growth. If you want additional exercises, please consider our series of workbooks, available online at www.thecircle blueprint.com.

Steps to Increase Self-Determination

1. Make a list of those areas where you are allowing someone or something else to determine your life choices. These could include your boss, spouse, friends.
2. Write next to each item on your list what you gain from not taking ownership of this area of your life. You might be avoiding conflict, responsibility, or risk.
3. Write next to each item what you stand to gain if you take over ownership of this area. You might become more independent, free, expressive.
4. Pick one item on your list that you are ready to own.
5. Express your intention to whomever or about whatever currently has control of you in this area.
6. Make yourself important enough to take over control of this issue. Don't let the fear of conflict or the opinions of others hold you back from making constructive change.

Steps to Increase Self-Efficacy

1. Notice where you lack confidence in your ability to have the life that you want. Make a list of whatever comes to mind.

2. Check to see if these areas where you aren't confident are important to you or if you think they should be important. If they aren't important to you, let them go.

3. Write down as clearly as you can what you understand your unique gift to be. If you are unclear, make a list of those things you do where you have the most success and from which you gain the most satisfaction.

4. Notice the power and success you have when you are doing what you love.

5. Begin to apply your power to the issues in your life where you want to succeed. In other words, consider how you approach the issues from your unique perspective and with your strengths.

Steps to Improve Zest

1. What did you do today that drained you of your energy? How can you avoid doing those things tomorrow?

2. When did you feel delight today? What were you doing? How can you do more of those things tomorrow?

3. If you followed your delight, where would it take you? What can you do to move in that direction?

4. List all the things you did today that engaged your creativity.

5. Design the perfect job to fit your creativity, bring you the greatest joy, and interest you the most.

6. See what you can do to alter your job to fit your perfect job.

Steps to Expand Acceptance

1. Notice where you are resisting what life is bringing to you, whether it is some change, opportunity, or obstacle.

2. Imagine what positive outcome might be on the other side of this change. If nothing positive comes to mind, be more creative.

3. Consider the thought that life is your friend and has good things in store for you. Remind yourself of this idea throughout the day.
4. Invite at least five people to give you feedback as to how they experience you, both good and bad. Accept whatever they say without resistance.
5. Extract one lesson from the feedback you receive and make a change based on that feedback.

Steps to Increase Your Self-Discipline

1. Make a list of goals that are important for you to achieve.
2. Next to each item on your list, write down what you need to do in order to achieve it. List the steps from what needs to be done first to the very last step. If you have many goals, pick only one or two for this exercise.
3. Make a list of temptations and distractions that you are likely to face as you move toward your goal.
4. Create a list of rewards you will give yourself for the successful completion of each small step in your plan.
5. Create a list of punishments you will impose on yourself when you stray.
6. Learn to accept that straying from your plan doesn't mean you have failed. Simply recommit to your goal and get started again.

Chapter 12

Humility

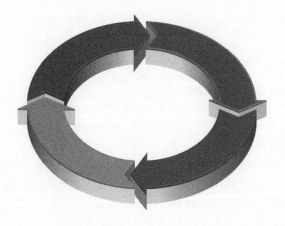

The Violet

Down in a green and shady bed,
A modest violet grew;
Its stalk was bent, it hung its head
As if to hide from view.

And yet it was a lovely flower,
Its colour bright and fair;
It might have graced a rosy bower,
Instead of hiding there.

Yet thus it was content to bloom,
In modest tints arrayed;
And there diffused a sweet perfume,
Within the silent shade.

Then let me to the valley go
This pretty flower to see;
That I may also learn to grow
In sweet humility.

—Jane Taylor

The dilemma of true humility is captured so well by Ms. Taylor. Can we possess all of our beauty in such a way that we are content living in a "green and shady bed"? Can we enjoy all of our greatness while being content with being ordinary? This may not be such an easy task!

The Humility Element

Humility is quite simple to understand. Merriam-Webster defines humility as "the quality or state of not thinking you are better than other people: the quality or state of being humble."

For the purpose of the Circle we will define humility as having an accurate opinion of your talents, accomplishments, and limitations and keeping them in perspective. Humility is eliminating your self-focus to the point of forgetting yourself.

We have determined that there are five factors that make up the humility domain.

1. Modesty is the absence of the need to have your accomplishments seen and valued by others. Instead, it is being content with the inner satisfaction of knowing you have done the right thing and/or that you did your best work. Modesty is the ability to see your value realistically and not by comparing yourself to others. Those high in modesty are confident enough in themselves to know their own value but also to know that even if their abilities are greater than those of others in some way, that does not make them better. People low in modesty like to show off their gifts and accomplishments. They think they know it all and will remind others of this fact often; they are "showy" about their abilities.

There is a phenomenon that psychologists refer to as "illusory superiority" or the "better than average effect." While it is mathematically impossible for most people to be above average given the average is, by definition the middle, when asked, people consistently believe they are above average. In one striking study, 94 percent of professors rated themselves as above average, and we've all heard the classic story that most drivers believe they are better than the average driver. Why? Why can't we be moderate in assessments of our own ability or accomplishments or value? Why do we instead, tend to overestimate our worth relative to others? When we do this, we rob others of their value and set ourselves up for inaccurate, and unnecessary, comparisons that lead to pain in various forms, and, at high levels, can become narcissism.

2. *Narcissism* is the tendency to be preoccupied with being special and feeling superior to others. Narcissism leads to self-focus; grandiose, and sometimes unrealistic dreams and expectations; a willingness to take excessive risk; and the need to prove one's superiority by external accomplishments like advanced degrees from the right schools, material possessions, titles, and pedigrees. Narcissism can lead to the exploitation of others and a manipulative interpersonal style. Highly narcissistic people have an excessive interest in, or even love of, themselves. They tend to have a high level of self-obsession, believing everyone wants to hear their stories or watch their actions, and they might even take offense when others do not give them the attention they expect. Those low in narcissism lack this over-the-top self-obsession and instead, are more neutral; they will share stories and actions but also listen to and watch others with an equal interest.

Perhaps you are familiar with the Greek myth of young Narcissus. One day Narcissus was walking in the woods when Echo, an Oread (mountain nymph), saw him, fell deeply in love and followed him. Narcissus sensed he was being followed and shouted, "Who's there?" Echo repeated, "Who's there?" She eventually revealed her identity and attempted to embrace him. He stepped away and told her to leave him alone. She was heartbroken and spent the rest of her life in lonely glens until nothing but an echo sound remained of her. Nemesis, the goddess of revenge, learned of this story and decided to punish Narcissus. She lured him to a pool where he saw his own reflection. He didn't realize it was only an image and fell in love with it. He eventually realized that his love could not be consummated and committed suicide.

This is such a common error in our world. Men and women come to see that which is special in themselves and become so enamored with themselves that they become the focus and center of their world. They become attached to being treated as if they are special and so demand such treatment wherever they go. They come to believe they deserve a certain standard of living to such a degree that if it is threatened or begins to fall away, they resort to all manner of deception to prop it up. They carry themselves with such swagger and exaggerated self-confidence that they are prone to excesses of every sort. Their preoccupation with their uniqueness distorts their ability to see how they might truly be most useful (and important) in the world.

We see examples of such distorted self-love in many areas of life. Divas and rock stars sometimes believe their own hype and come to expect to be adored by thronging fans. Professional sports figures can't accept retirement even when it is obvious their playing days have passed. CEOs, military leaders, and politicians begin to think that they are untouchable and can write their own rules for life. They become like big balloons filled with their self-aggrandizement that rise but only for a while. At some point, their distortion cannot be sustained and they fall to earth, often with tragic consequences for themselves and for others.

3. *Self-monitoring* is the ability to see oneself accurately and so to understand how effectively you are interacting with those around you. Consider a computer, television, or science monitor—a dictionary might define this as "a device for observing." It seems overly simple, perhaps, but that is a pretty accurate definition. All of us possess such a monitor for ourselves. We can observe our actions. Those higher in self-monitoring possess the ability to respond to what they see in that monitor and make corrections in response to the circumstances. They notice how others respond to what is being done or said and make adjustments when necessary, such as clarifying statements when it is clear that others do not understand something that they have said. Those lower in self-monitoring may not notice what they are observing or may not care, and, as a result, they do not make changes that are needed, given their observations.

The problem of lacking adequate self-monitoring is common enough to be the subject of Robert Sutton's interesting book with the unusual (and hopefully not too offensive) title, *The No Asshole Rule*. He asserts there are two tests for spotting someone acting like an asshole.

We all know people who lack proper self-monitoring. They are the people who stand too close to you when they talk and have no idea they are making you uncomfortable. They are the ones who talk too much at lunch and aren't aware that they leave no room for anyone else to speak. They say the most outlandish things and don't imagine that anyone would be offended. They just don't have a clue.

◆ Test One: After talking to the alleged asshole, does the "target" feel oppressed, humiliated, de-energized, or belittled by the person? In particular, does the target feel worse about him or herself?

◆ Test Two: Does the alleged asshole aim his or her venom at people who are *less powerful* rather than at those people who are more powerful?

Sutton goes on to list his "Dirty Dozen" common everyday actions that assholes use:

1. Personal insults
2. Invading one's "personal territory"
3. Uninvited physical contact
4. Threats and intimidation, both verbal and nonverbal
5. Sarcastic jokes and teasing used to insult delivery systems
6. Withering e-mail flames
7. Status slaps intended to humiliate their victims
8. Public shaming or "status degradation" rituals
9. Rude interruptions
10. Two-faced attacks
11. Dirty looks
12. Treating people as if they are invisible

Perhaps you have worked for someone like this. Or, perhaps you have treated others in some of these ways. It is not a pleasant experience to work for or with someone who is behaving in this manner. Developing the ability to self-monitor and catch ourselves going down a path toward these actions, and ultimately, stopping them before they occur, is a key aspect of humility.

4. *Self-esteem* is a word with two parts: self and esteem. In what level of esteem do you hold yourself? Those higher in self-esteem hold themselves in a healthy esteem, that is, they view themselves with a level of regard. They don't feel the need to prove anything to others, rather, they have confidence in their abilities and skills. They are confident in their value and their abilities without being narcissistic. Those with lower self-esteem are not confident that what they offer the world is enough, and instead, question their worth and value. They tend to feel inadequate. This can lead to many maladaptive behaviors such as concealing, pretending, and overcompensating. People with low self-esteem tend to imagine others are better than they are and become focused on others instead of placing their attention on their own journey.

Self-esteem is about loving yourself just the way you are. This seems so simple, yet it can be difficult to do. Inputs from media, friends, and our own thoughts constantly tell us to lose weight, make more money, be funnier, smarter, and so on. Gaining perspective and loving those things about ourselves that make us special is key to having good self-esteem.

5. *Tolerance* is the ability to be accepting of yourself and of others as well as of the situation you are in. People high in tolerance rarely, if ever, judge others. They make room for the differences of those around them, are accepting of mistakes, and are gracious in forgiving those who transgress against them. At the same time, they do not view circumstances that might be different from what they would like as unacceptable. Rather, they handle differences—with others—with a level of grace. People who are low on tolerance are just the opposite. They are quick to judge, slow to forgive, and open to take advantage of the weaknesses and mistakes of others to gain advantage. They also tend to act out, both toward others simply because they have differences like skin color or political beliefs and toward circumstances that are different from what they view as optimal.

A friend was riding on the elevated train into the city on a busy Tuesday morning. He had an important meeting and was dressed in his best suit. Gradually the train filled with commuters and every seat was taken. He offered his seat to an elderly African American woman. As he stood in that train car, he noticed that he was surrounded by people who looked very different from him. They were Hispanic laborers, young students on the way to class, and African American folks like the old lady. At first, he felt the differentness in their lives and he had a jolt of superiority. But, then the strangest thing happened. As he looked around, he had this overwhelming sense of belonging. These were people just like him. Everyone belongs to the same family. It was one of the best feelings he had ever had; the sense of belonging to a group of strangers whom he would never see again. He longs to live in that sense every day he lives.

Our friend discovered the value of tolerance and it changed him. He experienced humility in all of its wonderful power.

Three Models for Seeing Yourself

HUBRIS

Hubris is characterized as seeing yourself as bigger and more important than you are and being unable or unwilling to see your connectedness to or the true value of the world around you. You see hubris in those who overestimate their accomplishments and carry themselves with too much self-importance.

LOW SELF-ESTEEM

Low self-esteem is evident when we make others more important than they actually are and make ourselves either nonexistent or small. People stuck in low self-esteem fail to see their value and power. They overinflate the value of others, imaging that they need their support and assistance far more than they actually do.

HUMILITY

True humility is the full awareness of your unique gifts and full deployment of your strengths and power in the context of your essential and continuous connectedness to the life you share with all of

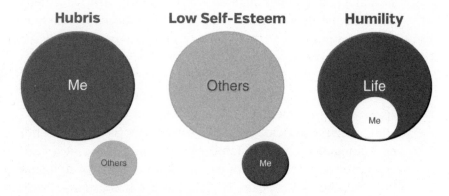

FIGURE 12.1   **Three Modes of Self-Esteem**

creation. It requires *relinquishing control*. The act of relinquishing control must come from a realization that you were never and will never be in control. For many, this realization only comes at the time when all of their inflated pretense is wiped away. When all of your gifts and talents, your youth, money, and power are gone it is much easier to grasp the true value of who you are. This is the reason to venerate the elderly. They can be a source of wisdom precisely because they are beyond the ego's deceit. They can see more clearly because they better comprehend their place in the grand scheme of life. At this stage of life, when we have been stripped of our boasting and pretense, we often find not defeat, frustration, and resentment but love, grace, peace, and acceptance. We are often left with a laughable sense that the things we thought were important in our younger days have little or no meaning at all.

Humility Chapter Summary

Humility is the quality or state of not thinking you are better than others. For the purpose of the Circle we have defined humility as having an accurate opinion of your talents, accomplishments, and limitations and keeping them in the biggest of all perspectives. Humility is eliminating your self-focus to the point of forgetting yourself in order to see your value in making a positive difference in the world around you.

Each of the five factors increase humility by:

♦ Acting with modesty, which includes reducing the need to be the center of attention, talking about yourself, and showing off in front of others. Understanding and looking for the reasons that you are just like everyone else, while also recognizing that you are special, will also increase humility for this factor.

♦ Being less narcissistic and increasing humility by focusing less on what makes you special and seeing yourself as being like everyone else. Understanding your similarity, not through comparison, but through simple values and common life needs and desires (e.g., affection, humor, sickness) is critical to expanding humility. Standing in line, waiting your turn, listening before expressing your needs, hard manual labor (e.g., yard work), and avoiding taking advantage of those less fortunate (e.g., intellectually, physically, financially) will increase humility and reduce narcissistic tendencies.

♦ Increasing self-awareness is the first step toward increasing humility through self-monitoring behaviors. These behaviors allow you to progress toward balance through effective internal feedback. Only when you can see yourself accurately and choose how you show up in the world around you can you grow and mature.

♦ Increasing your comfort level with yourself builds self-esteem, which increases levels of humility. Strong self-esteem reduces the need to boast or show off to prove your sense of being adequate. Knowing your strengths and taking responsibility for your decisions also increases self-esteem and, thus, humility.

♦ Increasing tolerance for others increases humility. This includes trusting others, forgiving others for their transgressions, and seeing your own weaknesses rather than judging the weaknesses and shortcomings of others. Tolerance is about acceptance, kindness, and grace.

Each of the same five factors can decrease your humility by:

1. Acting without modesty by being arrogant, bragging, and standing out in the crowd and talking about yourself reduces humility. Similarly, having a lack of appreciation for the good things that have happened in your life and the grace you have received interferes with your ability to develop humility.

2. Confronting narcissism is a normal part of our development. Young children tend to be narcissistic when they first encounter their independence. We call it the "terrible twos." Teenagers tend to be narcissistic as they seek their own identity and become wrapped up in themselves. Adult narcissism is a bigger issue, especially when it persists and resists being tempered. Narcissistic/Machiavellian tendencies that reduce humility include believing things are owed to you, expecting special treatment, and manipulating others to achieve your personal goals; these significantly reduce humility.

3. Lacking self-monitoring behaviors—including a lack of self-awareness, poor ability to control your emotions, and impulsive and reckless acting out to attain your wants and needs—stand in the way of the cultivation of mature humility.

4. Feeling sorry for yourself, being overly harsh toward yourself, and refusing to take 100 percent responsibility for your choices and their outcomes reduce self-esteem and undermine true humility. Low self-esteem masquerades as humility, but true humility is built on the foundation of self-confidence and faith in oneself.

5. Having low regard for those in need, believing that an eye for an eye is just, and lacking the desire to forgive all reduce tolerance for others and humility. A high level of tolerance leads to the opportunity for grace, which is the pinnacle of humility.

Questions to Better Understand Your Mastery of Humility

◆ Of whom are you jealous? What motivates you to want what they have?

◆ Are you taking credit for anything for which you are not truly responsible? Are you willing to give it up?

◆ How do you identify yourself? Is it in your uniqueness or in that which you have in common with others?

◆ Where do you show kindness and care for others?

◆ Do people experience you as caring or do they find you difficult and overbearing?

◆ What have you learned from your failure and loss?

◆ When do you most easily find yourself connected to the world?

◆ How could you expand your service to the world?

◆ Who are you trying to make small to make yourself seem bigger?

◆ How are you disrespectful, neglectful, or abusive to those around you?

◆ How could you shift to create a positive and uplifting impact?

Note: Please feel free to tear out this page for reference as you work through this chapter.

Humility

Humility is quite simple to understand. Merriam-Webster defines humility as "the quality or state of not thinking you are better than other people; the quality or state of being humble." For the purpose of the Circle we will define humility as having an accurate opinion of your talents, accomplishments, and limitations and keeping them in perspective. Humility is eliminating your self-focus to the point of forgetting yourself.

- ◆ Modesty
  The absence of the need to have your accomplishments seen and valued by others. Modesty is the ability to see your value realistically and not by comparing yourself to others.
- ◆ Narcissism
  The tendency to be preoccupied with being special and feeling superior to others. Narcissism can lead to the exploitation of others and a manipulative interpersonal style.
- ◆ Self-Monitoring
  The ability to see oneself accurately and so to understand how effectively you are interacting with those around you.
- ◆ Self-Esteem
  Reflects a person's overall subjective emotional evaluation of his or her own utility. When self-esteem is high, you feel good about yourself.
- ◆ Tolerance
  The ability or willingness to allow the existence of opinions or behavior that one does not necessarily agree with. People high in tolerance rarely, if ever, judge others.

ACTION STEP ONE

Now that you have completed the chapter on humility, please return to www.thecircleblueprint.com to complete the assessment. Once you have completed it, you will receive the results to review before progressing to Chapter 13: Purpose. Alternately, you may choose to substitute honest self-reflection on each element.

ACTION STEP TWO

After you take the assessment, turn your attention to the following exercises. We offer exercises for each factor. In areas where you are not thriving, there is room for growth. If you want additional exercises, please consider our series of workbooks, available online at www.thecircleblueprint.com.

Steps to Increase Modesty Behaviors

1. Notice when are extolling your own virtues. Ask yourself what drives you to do so and if you can be content simply being yourself.
2. Choose to not make yourself the center of attention. Instead, make others the focus of your attention.
3. Delight in the ordinary parts of yourself and the ways you are like everyone else. Look for and appreciate the common ground between yourself and others.
4. Be aware of feelings of superiority. Once aware of these feelings, work to avoid them. If you're smarter, that's fine; this doesn't make you better than any other person. Recognize that your unique gifts may make you special and more capable than others in some ways, but that others have gifts that make them more capable than you in other ways.

Steps to Reduce Narcissistic Behaviors

1. Become more aware of your narcissistic tendencies. Notice when you find yourself feeling superior to those around you or when you expect to be treated in a special manner. Challenge those thoughts with the ways you are similar to others.

2. Become a better listener. A core deficit that defines narcissistic behavior is self-centeredness. Listening to others will be of great help in reducing your narcissistic tendencies. Practice reframing what you are hearing to check if you are hearing others accurately.

3. Consider how you can use your gifts and talents for the betterment of humanity. Focus your gifts on making the world a better place instead of using them for your own benefit.

4. Focus on expressing your love and care as often as possible. Narcissists keep a cool distance. They avoid being open and vulnerable. Practice serving those around you in practical ways. Jesus washed the feet of his disciples. He did so as a lesson in leadership. He who wants to be the leader of all must become the servant of all. What a powerful lesson!

Steps to Improve Self-Monitoring

1. Create a relationship with a trusted adviser. This is one of the primary values of an executive or life coach. Powerful people sometimes have great difficulty finding someone who will give them honest feedback. So many people benefit from pleasing the boss by reflecting his greatness that they would never dream of telling the emperor that he is wearing no clothes. A trusted adviser will give honest, candid feedback in real time.

2. Instead of measuring yourself against the reflection of greatness you receive from others, create clear performance metrics tied to concrete goals. Gain your feedback from what you actually accomplish rather than from flattery.

3. Understand where pride is your enemy. Pay attention to phrases like "What's done is done," or "She will get over it." These are clear indications that you have done something that your pride is trying to cover up. You have likely overstepped your bounds and your unconscious self is aware of your misdeed.

Steps to Improve Self-Esteem

1. Notice when you are comparing yourself to others. Ask yourself what you are learning about yourself by the comparison. Gently shift your focus to noticing your strengths and weaknesses without judging yourself as better or worse than others.
2. Take stock of your strengths and weaknesses. Create a composite that includes both and consider how that mix equips you to have an effective and meaningful life.
3. Create goals that fit your unique complement of strengths and weaknesses. How can you expand and develop your unique life?
4. It is okay to admire great qualities in others without feeling less than they. Begin by complimenting and appreciating the qualities you value in others. This will ease your need to compete.
5. Above all else, don't try to be perfect. No one is.

Steps to Improve Tolerance

1. Take a few minutes to recall those who showed tolerance to you. Remember the benefit you received from being accepted and forgiven when it was not merited. Consider the benefit you gained from the tolerance of others. Now consider the benefit you can bring to others in your life by showing tolerance to them.
2. Notice how your judgments create division. Practice looking beyond your judgments to that which you and your adversaries have in common. What are you both trying to achieve? Is there a way you can get there together? Learn to look at all situations through the lens of tolerance.

Chapter 13

Purpose

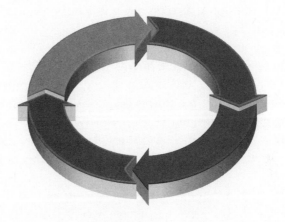

The Road Not Taken

Two roads diverged in a yellow wood,
And sorry I could not travel both
And be one traveler, long I stood
And looked down one as far as I could
To where it bent in the undergrowth;
Then took the other, as just as fair,
And having perhaps the better claim,
Because it was grassy and wanted wear;
Though as for that the passing there
Had worn them really about the same,
And both that morning equally lay
In leaves no step had trodden black.

Oh, I kept the first for another day!
Yet knowing how way leads on to way,
I doubted if I should ever come back.
I shall be telling this with a sigh
Somewhere ages and ages hence:
Two roads diverged in a wood, and I—
I took the one less traveled by,
And that has made all the difference.

—Robert Frost

Our lives are a one-way street. Each day we make choices that create our path, our journey. Seemingly small choices sometimes shape major changes that alter the course of our lives. You turned left at the light and were blindsided by a drunk driver. What if you had turned right? You took that job that required you to uproot and move. The company rocketed to wild success and your equity means you don't have to work another day for the rest of your life. What if you had passed on that job for the one that was near home?

You invest your time and energy every day in something. You make choices because of the things you consider important. But are they truly the most important things in which to invest? Are you sure?

The retailer Sears used to have three levels for each of its appliances: good, better, and best. Have you chosen the best road for your life?

Which road have you chosen in the woods of your life? Does it make a difference? We agree with Frost's words, "And that has made all the difference." It is the finding of the "best road" for your life that we refer to as purpose. Purpose is about seeing the truth about life and thus living each moment in the context of that truth and in the pursuit of that truth. Please pause for a moment and consider the importance of this idea. All of the choices you make every day are based on the context of what you see and know. Are you making the choices that help you down your best road?

The Purpose Element

Purpose is a clear understanding of how to deploy your giftedness in the most useful manner. Your gifts were given to you as an investment that expects a return; they were not given to you only to be used to create your own success and to secure your life. If you use your talents in so small a way, you are missing the bigger picture. When you see the difference you can make in the world, you will be playing the big game—and it is quite likely that your life will be more abundant as a result.

There are six factors that make up the purpose domain:

1. *Resolve.* This construct describes the trait of clearly knowing your destination before your start your journey, thoughtfully determining your progress, and the ability to choose wisely. Stephen R. Covey in his classic leadership book, *7 Habits of Highly Effective People*, refers to these qualities when he writes, "'Begin with the end in mind' is based on the principle that all things are created twice. There's a mental or first creation, and a physical or second creation to all things." (Covey 1989) Those who have cultivated these skills move thoughtfully and deliberately through life. They do not waver in their pursuit of their purpose and will not settle for less than achieving their purpose. They have a stick-to-itiveness that makes them resolute in their pursuit of their best road—they make a definitive decision and they simply do it, purposefully. Those who lack these skills, however, meander through their lives without much of a sense of where they are going or how they will get there. They expend wasted effort on choices that don't advance in any useful direction and tend to bend easily to a difficulty or obstacle and thus, get off track in their intended pursuits.

Resolve plays out in many ways. You buy the laundry soap you believe will best clean your clothes. You date the very best guy or girl you know. You have the best job you think you can get. But the world is a big place. There might be a much better laundry soap, guy, girl, and job out there. So are you settling for less than you could have?

Of course, the issue is much bigger than laundry soap. This is your life. Are you living into all of the meaning your life could have? What if there is much more for you than you see today? What might you be missing? Resolve now to pursue the much more, not to miss out on the purpose, stay on your best road.

2. *Diligence.* Diligence involves deliberately and persistently acting in pursuit of a goal. Taking care of your own affairs, remaining calm under pressure, and avoiding impulsive behavior are all important to achieving what you want. Diligence requires the ability to pay attention to important details and to follow through on successive tasks that advance your goals. Both aid in cultivating purpose. Those high in diligence will operationalize their purpose with consistent, steadfast effort toward goals worthy of their lives. They will not stop and start continuously and change the goal over and over; they keep working until they achieve that which they desire. Those who lack diligence simply don't pay adequate attention to all that is going on in their lives, and their efforts to attain goals are shaky at best. They miss important clues and/or lack the interest or personal discipline to stick with their plans. Life is often providing us feedback that, when overlooked or ignored, requires us to repeat the same lessons until we are willing to pay attention. As a result, those low in diligence tend not to reach the goal or purpose, because they cannot sustain effort or focus on the goal long enough.

> *I really don't know what you mean by climbing to the top of the mountain. My days are a grind. I am busy from the time I open my eyes until I close them again. I don't have time to think about my life. It is difficult enough just to survive. I often feel like one of those hamsters that runs on the wheel every day. If I don't run, I can't pay the bills. I certainly don't feel like I am getting anywhere. Life is hard. That's just the way it is.*

Our friend is not alone. Many people are simply surviving or enduring their lives. The way they view their lives leads them to live that way. Acting with deliberateness and diligence requires seeing what is truly important and then steadfastly, persistently, patiently pursuing that goal until you have achieved it. Most of what is truly valuable in life requires deliberateness and diligence. No one mastered the violin or became a champion diver without exercising deliberateness and diligence. Similarly, no one built a truly great life without cultivating those same qualities. Steadfast, unwavering, and committed application of your time and energy in pursuit of your goals is required to get anywhere that is worthwhile.

3. *Myopia.* The medical condition of myopia is often called near-sightedness and at extreme levels, means people can only see objects very close to their face and even when looking at, say, a picture, can only see a portion of it at a time. The concept of myopia with respect to purpose is similar. Those who are highly myopic have a very narrow view and cannot see anything bigger or more meaningful. They are often closed-minded and lack the ability to see beyond a single focus. Those who are less myopic can see a bigger picture and even extend their sight to imagine new opportunities. Their minds, and views, are open and broad.

Imagine you were looking through a cardboard tube with your other eye closed and we asked you what you see. You could describe what you see quite well. And what you were seeing would be real and accurate. But it would be but a very small subset of all there was to see. If you were basing your decisions and actions on that small slice of reality, your likelihood of making wise ones would be quite small.

Sometimes blinders are put on horses to limit their peripheral vision. This is useful if they are pulling a wagon or operating in crowded and congested areas where they might be easily spooked. But being able to see only what is front of them limits their ability to react to any danger that comes from the side. They are completely defenseless.

You are building your life on what you see. What if there is much, much more of which you are not aware? Your judgment and decisions must be hopelessly flawed.

One place that limited vision shows up frequently is in how we see ourselves.

I don't know what is wrong with my team. Each of them is so bright and capable but they simply won't make decisions. I keep telling them that we need to move quickly. They can't do it. When we meet they seem to agree with me. But when we meet a few days later they have changed their minds. I am so frustrated. Sometimes, I want to give up. How can I lead them if they won't follow?

Our friend is deeply disturbed. He sees himself as a committed leader of the team who is doing all he can to create the success they all want. But when you talk to his teammates, they see it differently. They describe their leader as pushy, abrasive, and toxic. They don't like being pushed into the things he thinks are important, but he does it all the time.

What's going on here? The leader is looking through a tube. He is only seeing his intentions. He is blind to the negative impact he is creating on the people he is trying to lead. Unless he becomes aware of the bigger reality, it is unlikely this team will stay together. A good project will be derailed because he is blind to the consequences of his behavior.

We all do this all the time. Some of us see through a tube that is so constricting that the choices that make sense to us are actually so outside the norm that we are put into jail or committed to a hospital. Most of us have a sufficiently large tube as to make socially responsible choices most of the time. We can see with relative clarity the impact of our decisions and how they will be received by others. But there is so much we might not be seeing.

4. *Experience sharing.* The creation and telling of stories is part of the fabric of the human condition. Stories are no more than the meaning we make of the events in our lives. Our stories are, to some extent, always shaped by our past experiences and biases. We move toward purpose when our stories inspire us to bring our best selves into our work and lives, when they support our understanding that our lives matter and that we can make a difference in the world. Our stories undermine our purpose when they limit our ability to see the bigger picture and so lead us into insecurity, selfishness, greed, envy, prejudice, and bigotry. Just as the right stories can make us big, the wrong stories can make us petty and small. The quality of our stories shapes how we live and how we influence those around us. They become the filter through which we understand the people in our life and, to the extent that the filter is biased, so too are all of our judgments and reactions.

Hold the truth (facts) tightly. But, hold your stories lightly. Understand that your stories are more likely to be wrong than right because they are based on limited data. Stories constrict your vision and make it difficult, if not impossible, to see the bigger picture. We must learn to see beyond the grip of our stories. As we let in more information, our judgments and behaviors will change along with them.

I had a chip on my shoulder because I was passed over for a promotion last year and didn't get a raise. It didn't seem fair. I had been counting on that extra money and, when I didn't get it, I felt like I had to count every penny before I bought anything. I came to see that I had enough money and that I was actually creating the sense of unfairness that was fueling my resentment. It was as if my eyes suddenly opened and I saw my world very differently. I had been creating my own obstacles. I was resenting people who truly valued me and wanted me on their team. I had been considering leaving a place where I was making a significant and valuable contribution and for no good reason. Almost immediately, I saw opportunities to expand my impact. I began working more collaboratively with those same people I had resisted. I was a lot happier and I think it showed to others. In fact, within a few months I was promoted and given a significant raise. It's funny because the raise didn't mean nearly as much as I had expected it to. I guess the whole issue with the money was only the result of the story I had created about being treated unfairly. When I got out of the grip of the story, I felt free ... and my life worked a lot better.

Our friend was rapidly heading down a dead-end street and didn't know it. In fact, it made sense to him to be on that road. It was only when he got out of the grip of his story that a whole new path appeared to him. He was a very fortunate man. So many people never question their stories and so never know there is another path—one filled with better options and opportunities.

This is our hope for you, that you will see what you can't currently see about your life. We want you to identify where you are stuck and the stories that keep you stuck in that place. This is how you will begin to see a bigger picture, one that has many more options for you than you can now see.

One way to learn to hold your stories lightly is to generate alternative stories that can explain the same facts.

My wife and I have a habit of kissing each other hello when we come into the house. One day I was standing at the kitchen sink and I heard the garage door opening. A few minutes later my wife came up the stairs and walked right by without kissing me. At first I was surprised. We always kiss each other hello. After a few minutes my surprise began to morph into a bit of anger. "Why didn't she kiss me?" I wondered. "Maybe she's angry." But, for what reason is she angry? It was her birthday last week and I bought a nice gift and took her to her favorite restaurant for dinner. Now, I am getting pretty steamed. "She's angry for no reason at all. I hate this about her." I hear her coming down the stairs but I don't want to be around her and so I go to the basement. I'm down there kicking stuff around venting my frustration when she comes looking for me. "What's the matter with you?" she asks. "What's the matter with me?" I say. "What's the matter with you?" And we got into a big fight.

How much better would it have been if, when she didn't kiss me, I took a few minutes to realize I was getting trapped in the grip of my story that she was angry at me and generated a few alternate stories instead? "Maybe she had to go to the bathroom." "Perhaps she had a gift for me that she was hiding." "Maybe something happened at work and she is upset and preoccupied." Any of these could be true, I realized. Now when I hear her coming down the stairs, I ask her, "Honey, you didn't kiss me when you came in, are you angry?" "Of course not," she replies. "I just had to go to the bathroom. Traffic was terrible." Now, we have a great night together.

Learn to generate alternative stories. They can be of great benefit to avoid silly conflicts and create opportunities for harmony and peace.

5. *Self-deception* is the act of misleading oneself. Nothing could be more damaging in the pursuit of purpose than to fool yourself about what you are doing and why you are doing it. History is filled with the stories of world leaders who imagined they were pursuing great goals while committing monstrous atrocities. Were they so blind they could not see what they were doing? Only if we possess the ability to be

honest with ourselves can we cultivate our true purpose. Those who are high in self-deception mislead themselves and have no ability to accurately assess their motives or the impact of their actions. Those who are low in self-deception see themselves clearly and are honest about what they see. They know what drives their choices and understand the consequences of their behavior.

Perhaps the greatest source of self-deception is one we all share: the ego. Everyone has an ego. Your ego is that voice in your head that is always evaluating and judging everything. If you don't realize you have one, stop reading and pay attention to the thoughts running through your mind.

The ego arises to answer one simple and profound question: "Who am I?" The ego invites you to answer that question by looking at the outside of your life. Are you tall or short? Pretty or plain? Popular or not so much? Do you live in a big, expensive house or a small, modest one? From all of these comparisons your ego determines your worth. You are better than your neighbor if your car is more expensive than his. You are better than your buddy if you got into a more prestigious school. You are better than the other girls at school because you have more friends than anyone else has.

It is this self-deception that leads to all kinds of trouble. Jealousy, envy, gossip, competition, lies, fighting, and war all result from following the ego's path of establishing your worth by comparing yourself to others.

The truth lies in a very different direction. Who you are has little to nothing to do with your appearance, accomplishments, or possessions. Who you really are is that which occupies your body— the inner you. When you see your inner you clearly and identify your value with it, you will discover a deep sense of humility and an opening to purpose that will guide you to your greatness.

6. *Spirituality.* Spirituality is not referring to any religion or religious practice. Instead, it is about seeing that life is much bigger and more complex than that which is material. Of course, the material world is important. Much of our lives are filled with obtaining, managing, and consuming material things. But there are qualities in life that are not material in any way and are absolutely fundamental to purpose. Consider such things as love, beauty, kindness, generosity, forgiveness, joy, and peace. None of these can be bought or sold. None can be stored up in banks or set aside for retirement. Those who are high in spirituality have learned how to cultivate those spiritual qualities, which become more valuable than material things. Those who are low in spirituality may not even acknowledge the existence of anything beyond the material and, while they certainly experience and value spiritual qualities, they lack the understanding of how to source them in their lives.

> I was so busy that it seemed my head was always down focused on the next thing on my to-do list. I like being busy and having a lot to do gave me the feeling that I was valuable and important. Two months ago, I was on my way home from the gym and felt a terrible pain shooting down my arm. I thought I must have hurt myself at the gym, but when I woke up in the hospital and was told it was a heart attack, everything changed. I was told I had to slow down, reduce my stress, and have a more balanced life. I started taking walks and noticing things that in my busyness I had missed. I began to see the beauty in the sunrise on my way to work and in the sunset as I sat on my back porch after dinner. It was amazing! How could I have missed such beauty? I began to wonder about the source of beauty and the enormity of the universe. It seems peculiar to me that I had never slowed down enough to consider how much happens to support my life that has nothing to do with me. The earth travels through space at amazing speed. The sun rises and sets. The rain falls. Food grows. All of this is the context of my life. I expend no effort in any of these amazing things. At the same time, my life depends on all of them. Because I had slowed down and now saw such amazing wonder, I developed a new sense of appreciation for the gift of life. I know this was good for me. I am much more at peace with myself and my world. I connect with others in a richer way. I hate to say that my heart attack was good for me, but in a very real way it opened my eyes to the "more" that I had missed.

It took a crisis to open the eyes of the woman in this story. The wonder of life had always been present, but she had been moving too fast to notice. She took her busyness as evidence that she was living a truly big life when, in fact, it was distracting her from seeing what is truly big.

It is easy to confuse achieving with having purpose. It takes a great deal of effort and talent to run a business, raise a family, or master the violin. Certainly, achievement is useful, valuable, and should be celebrated. But purpose is bigger than achievement. It requires seeing yourself in the grandest context of all: the world of spirit. When you see who you really are and what you can really do, you will add a sense of meaning to all of your activities and achievements that will transform you.

Note: Please feel free to tear out this page for reference as you work through this chapter.

Purpose

Our lives are a one-way street. Each day we make choices that create our path, our journey. Seemingly small choices sometimes shape major changes that alter the course of our lives. You turned left at the light and were blindsided by a drunk driver. What if you had turned right? You took that job that required you to uproot and move. The company rocketed to wild success and your equity means you don't have to work another day for the rest of your life. What if you had passed on that job for the one that was near home? You invest your time and energy every day in something. You make choices because of the things you consider important. But, are they truly the most important things in which to invest? Are you sure? The retailer Sears used to have three levels for each of its appliances: good, better, and best. Have you chosen the best road for your life? Which road have you chosen in the woods of your life? Does it make a difference?

- ◆ Resolve
  The trait of clearly knowing your destination before you start your journey, thoughtfully determining your progress and the ability to choose wisely.
- ◆ Diligence
  Taking care of your own affairs, remaining calm under pressure, and avoiding impulsive behavior are all important in acting with deliberateness.
- ◆ Myopia
  The degree to which we are teachable, see the big picture, and allow our point of view to be shaped by perspective and balance.
- ◆ Experience Sharing
  The creation and telling of stories is part of the fabric of the human condition. We move toward purpose when our stories inspire us.
- ◆ Self-Deception
  A critical key to purpose because it can lead us onto a path that is pointed in the opposite direction from where we intend to go.
- ◆ Spirituality
  Spirituality simply acknowledges that the universe is bigger than you. It is a necessary component to finding your true purpose.

Purpose Chapter Summary

Each day you make choices that create your path, your journey. Seemingly small choices sometimes shape major changes that alter the course of your life. You invest your time and energy every day in something. You make choices because of the things you consider important. But are they truly the most important things in which to invest? Have you chosen the best road for your life?

Each of the six factors can increase your purpose through:

1. Being resolute is the skill of picking the best goal for your life and then steadily moving toward it. It requires great wisdom to discern the goal worthy of your life (your purpose) and great determination to make it the center of your choices and actions.

2. Diligence is the skill of steadily progressing toward your purpose despite obstacles, challenges, and temptations to stray. Without diligence it is difficult to reach your potential and fulfill your purpose.

3. Myopia is the inability to see the big picture. You can't find your purpose if you are stuck in the weeds, focused on the small things that fill up each day. Purpose is a huge idea. You must be willing to open yourself to big thoughts and ideas to find it.

4. Experience sharing is the ability to put your perspective into stories that you tell yourself and share with others. Stories shape how we see our world. They can be stories that weaken you or ones that inspire you toward your greatness.

5. Self-deception is the inclination to fool yourself about your own motives and actions. Only by seeing what is true about ourselves can we find our right path, the one where we are most useful and fulfilled.

6. Spirituality is the ability to see beyond the material to the world of spirit. Spiritual things like love, beauty, kindness, joy, and peace point the way to where your true purpose will be found.

Each of the same six factors also can decrease your purpose in the following ways:

1. Those who aren't sufficiently resolute will settle for a life that is less meaningful that it could have been. They will lack either the vision to see that life or the fortitude to pursue it.

2. Those who aren't sufficiently diligent will be too easily distracted from pursuing their purpose by competing goals and other interests. They are likely to stall when they encounter difficulties and obstacles.

3. Those who are myopic will fail to see the big picture that is the context for discovering their purpose. They are likely to be preoccupied with minor issues and petty concerns.

4. Those whose stories make them feel inadequate or lead them to be jealous of or judgmental toward others will be hampered in understanding their purpose. Their stories don't inspire them to see the very best within them.

5. Self-deception is one of the worst errors a person can make because it prevents you from seeing the truth about your own heart. You may not even know you are on the wrong path until it is too late to do much about it.

6. Those who lack interest in or the capacity for spirituality are not receptive to the spiritual qualities such as love, goodness, and joy that point toward ultimate purpose. Until you allow yourself to be guided by such values, you are cut off from deeper meaning.

ACTION STEP ONE

Now that you have completed the chapter on purpose, please return to www.thecircleblueprint.com to complete the assessment. Once you complete it, you will receive the results to review before progressing to Chapter 14: Balancing Purpose within the Circle. Alternately, substitute honest self-reflection on each element.

ACTION STEP TWO

After you take the assessment, focus on the exercises that follow. We offer exercises for each factor. In areas where you are not thriving, there is room for growth. If you want additional exercises, please

consider our series of workbooks, available online at www.thecircle
blueprint.com.

Steps to Improve Being Resolute

1. Write a statement that defines your current purpose. Are you satisfied with it?
2. Write a statement that describes what you believe is your true purpose.
3. Make a list of steps you would take to transition to your true purpose.
4. Make a list of obstacles you might encounter in that transition.
5. Remind yourself that you have a gift and a responsibility to use that gift in a big way.

Steps to Improve Diligence

1. Take 100 percent responsibility to make your life all that it should be.
2. List areas of your life for which you are not currently taking full responsibility.
3. Prioritize that list and begin taking ownership of each area.
4. List habits or behaviors that are getting in the way of you being your very best.
5. Begin changing those habits and stopping those behaviors.
6. Keep in mind each day the amazing life you are building.

Steps to Overcome Myopic Behavior

1. Keep track of times you get mired in pettiness.
2. Notice how often you waste time in mindless activities.
3. Take time to notice the beauty in nature.
4. Make a list of ways nature supports your life that you often overlook.
5. Make a list of the biggest questions you have about life. Can you think of bigger ones?
6. Invite a friend to discuss her view of the purpose of your life.

Steps to Improve Experience Sharing

1. Write down three stories about yourself.
2. Write down three stories about someone with whom you don't get along well.
3. Notice how strongly you believe these stories.
4. Generate alternative stories about yourself and the person with whom you don't get along well.
5. Practice holding your stories lightly.
6. Create three stories about yourself that inspire you to be greater.

Steps to Reduce Self-Deception

1. Make a list of your five greatest achievements.
2. Write down the motive behind each one.
3. Share your list with three people you trust and ask if they agree with your assessment.
4. Ask five people their honest view of your three greatest strengths and three greatest weaknesses.
5. Notice when you feel defensive and seek to identify what you might not be willing to face.

Steps to Increase Spirituality

1. Train yourself to notice every occurrence of spiritual qualities, such as love, joy, peace, patience, gentleness, and generosity.
2. Pay attention to those same spiritual qualities in your own heart.
3. Practice exercising those qualities in your interactions with others.
4. Consider how you can use your unique giftedness to create the greatest amount of goodness in the world.
5. Give more of your material wealth to those in need.

Chapter 14

Balancing Purpose within the Circle

Balance

Perhaps everyone desires purpose in their lives. But it seems that many find poor substitutes for the truest purpose life can provide. Real purpose requires the expansion and balance of your Circle.

No one can find their true purpose in life as long as their focus is only on themselves. Such a constricted view of one's life is simply too small to contain all that you were meant to be. You must learn to see the value you bring to others, to the redemption and renewal of the world, and to the expansion of goodness and beauty in the universe to find your true value. Until you see your purpose in the context of other aspects of the Circle to bring it into balance, it is impossible to expand your Circle and see yourself fully and accurately. You must master *and* balance the four fundamental elements of a mature life.

Each of the four aspects of the Circle builds on, and is built upon, the others. Until you have mastered independence, you cannot know your true giftedness. Without independence, your pursuit of security and significance is thwarted by your attempt to appear to be what those around you expect of you. You are a pretender rather than the independent soul you were created to be. Once you have found your independence, you are ready to discover your true power. You have a gift, some quality given to you that is the engine meant to drive your life. That quality is the source of your dignity, security, and purpose in the world. When you find it, you will begin to experience a new sense of significance and purposefulness. Your power prepares you to master humility. Humility opens your eyes to your connectedness to the world around you. It is only when you have gained humility that you begin to see the larger application of your power, because you learn that your gift was given as a stewardship. It was given to you to share to others. Your humility is the foundation for you to discover your connectedness to a higher power. As you seek to see your life and the world through these eyes, you finally are able to see clearly. You see things in their proper context. You begin to see the glory of your life and its most profound purpose.

Each of these four key elements is meant to balance the others. When one is mastered without the contribution of the others, distortion replaces wisdom.

Without independence, power will be wasted. Your gift will never shine as it was intended because it will be held back by the inclination to use it to please others. If you have not yet mastered independence, your purpose will be dwarfed by your need to satisfy and please those around you. Being a source of light in the world requires you to be bold, even to the point of facing rejection in order to stand for what is truly in the best interest of others. This is simply not possible for people who are building their lives on the need to please.

If you have not found your real power, you have not yet discovered your unique way of bringing light into the world. The power of your presence in transforming your life and the lives of others is fully connected to your unique gift. You simply must know who you were meant to be and what you were meant to do if you are going to fully connect to your true purpose. Without power, humility cannot be experienced, because true humility can never be built on a foundation of weakness. It is only when you know your power that you can begin to see how useful it is in the service of others. Humility without power is a pretense that is only a show on the outside while the inside of the person is filled with resentment, judgment, and bitterness.

If you have not yet learned humility, your life will be too much about yourself for you to truly understand and care for the needs of others. You will be seeking the light to shine on you rather than being the light to those who need it. Until you see your oneness with the world, your value to bring goodness will be limited indeed.

Many successful people feel hollow despite their success. Their outward success has not fulfilled their need to have real purpose in their lives. While they have the respect of the world for their accomplishments, power, and possessions, they know there is something more, something they have yet to find in life. They certainly have gained independence and may very well have found their power but they lack humility and purpose.

> *For years I ran a middle-market services firm. As the CEO, I employed over 500 full-time and another 1,000 variable-time employees. The company provided IT field maintenance and help desk services for national retailers. For the two decades I ran the company I longed for a job that provided more purpose and meaning. I had friends who were doctors, worked in nonprofits, and so on. I always thought that my role lacked meaning. I thought, if the cash registers didn't get fixed in a four-hour time frame for XX dollars would it really matter? Yet I made a good living, had a lot of responsibility, and met my personal commitments to my family by being the CEO of this company.*
>
> *Eventually I came to understand through countless interactions with my employees that my efforts and the company's success over the years provided great meaning to their lives. Many had gone to college, been promoted, bought homes, raised families, and even hired their family members into the company. At a very deep level the company provided a great benefit to many in society. The significance and meaning for them was obvious. This purpose and meaning did not translate easily to me, however. I always felt that if I had greater remuneration through more equity, control, and so on, I would have the freedom to leave the company and accomplish something more meaningful. Of course, I could leave at any time. My path to personal purpose and meaning was blocked by my lack of balance between the independence and power constructs of what I came to know as the Circle.*

Our friend was successful, but unsatisfied. He knew there was something missing from his life despite his success. He felt trapped even when he actually had quite a bit of freedom. He felt frustrated, even though he was creating value. Despite the fact that he was improving the lives of others, his life wasn't complete. He needed to break free from his need to meet the needs of others and find his true gifts in order to ascend to that place where his heart would be complete and satisfied.

It is our hope that if you feel that something is missing in your life these thoughts might be helpful to you. There are many people who want to know the "more" for their lives. It is our desire to be your guides. We want to help you be bright lights that bring goodness into every dark corner of this world.

Chapter 15

Achieving Greatness

Pulling It All Together

You have now completed your Circle Blueprint assessment, whether online or through self-reflection, and should have a pretty good idea of those aspects that you have mastered and the ones that will require some attention. You should be proud of having cultivated those aspects of greatness that are robust in your Circle. They are likely to be the very attributes that are the foundation of your current success and of the positive difference you are making in the lives of those around you.

At the same time, those traits that are underdeveloped are showing you precisely where you are limiting your greatness and where you have work to do. The exercises we provided at the end of previous chapters are only intended to be pointers toward the work you need to embrace. We know you will want more assistance and guidance.

To that end, we have created workbooks that expand on each of the four key elements necessary to have a robust and healthy Circle. In those workbooks you will find the step-by-step instruction necessary to continue to expand your Circle and your impact. We encourage you to continue the journey you have started. The wise man puts to use everything he learns in life. The fool is attracted to new ideas but never does anything with them. Choose to be wise. More information about the workbooks can be found at www.thecircleblueprint.com.

Ascending Your Throne

Our purpose in writing this book is to inspire you to believe in your innate greatness and to learn to feed and nurture that greatness for the good of the world and for your personal satisfaction. It is easy to spend your days and years being less that your very best self. We are surrounded by a world of people who have settled for mediocrity. Many of us were raised by people who lacked the vision to see who we truly are. Many of the habits we have developed serve only to maintain the status quo; they don't push us toward our greatness.

You cannot feed what you cannot see. Until you can see at least the smallest seeds of greatness in yourself, you cannot nurture and strengthen it.

We conclude this book with a variety of pictures that might help you see your greatness more clearly.

Picture 1: You Are Already Rich

You might imagine that money will make you rich. You might wish to live in a bigger home, to own a nicer car, to be able to afford a luxurious vacation. Aren't these the signs of being rich? Doesn't everyone want more of these things?

We have known too many people who are rich in material ways while being very poor in life.

Our friend in Chicago was the CEO of a Fortune 500 company. He was at the pinnacle of his career. He had risen through the ranks at some of the biggest and most successful companies in the world. He had been making a lot of money his whole career. He had a beautiful home on the North Shore—an upscale area of Chicago—and a lavish second home on a golf course in a swank resort in the South. He had arrived. He had the success, money, and influence everyone wants.

Right?

You would think he would have been one of the happiest and most contented men in the world. Not so! Despite his success, he was terrified. He had no tolerance for bad news. When his leadership team told him anything negative he would fly into a rage. He would turn beet red, the veins on his neck would stick out, and he would foam at the mouth such that spittle would land on the person to whom he was speaking. It was quite an unpleasant experience to disappoint this wealthy man. As we got to know him, we discovered that he had no sense of security with regard to his success. He worried about losing it all: his position, his wealth, his homes, and his reputation. He operated as if it was likely that he would be living in a cardboard box on Wacker Drive sometime in the not-too-distant future.

Despite the fact that we reminded him that his success was not an accident and that he was an exceptionally talented man, he was in the grip of a fear that robbed him of any sense of joy, peace, and security. His wealth had not made him rich. He was actually quite poor!

There is certainly nothing wrong with having money. But it is also true that money is not the source of true riches. Those who are truly rich understand that true riches come from the quality of your life. Money can buy things, but things do not create quality of life. This is one of the worst seductions in life.

So, we ask you, "What will it take for you to be rich?" If you immediately think of a long list of possessions that you must have to feel rich, you are on the wrong track. Instead, you might pause and consider all that you currently possess and realize you are already rich beyond measure.

- Do you have your health? What is that worth? Would you trade your health for any amount of money?
- Do you have people in your life who love you? Here is treasure money cannot buy.
- Do you have purpose in your life? Does your life matter to others? You are truly rich if you make a difference in the lives of others, whomever they might be.
- Do you have enough food for today, a roof over your head, clothes to wear? Then all of your needs are met. You need nothing.
- Did you have the opportunity to laugh today, to sing in the shower, to bring a smile to the face of a stranger?

You are already rich in so many ways. As you notice your true wealth, you will free up greater capacity for your greatness to expand.

Picture 2: You Are Truly a King or a Queen

Who do you see when you look in the mirror? If you see someone who is needy, weak, or inadequate in any way, you aren't seeing clearly. You need to look again. Do you know who you really are? You are a great king or queen. You have the ability to envision great things and to bring those things to life. You have power to rule your kingdom with wisdom and grace such that all around you thrive and are blessed. You possess riches beyond imagination and stores in your warehouses that cannot be exhausted. You have influence to sway the course of history, to end suffering, and to expand goodness. You are powerful in your character, a person of substance, someone whom others notice. People listen when you speak. They long to be around you. They take comfort in your leadership. They see their greatness in your empowerment. You bless the poor, heal the sick, bring justice to the downtrodden, and radiate blessing wherever you go. That is who you really are.

There was a time when you knew this about yourself, at least to some extent. When you were a child and dreamed of what you would be it was someone of importance, someone of value. Perhaps you would grow up to be the president, or a doctor, or an astronaut, or a professional athlete. You believed there was something special about you that would one day come to light.

Perhaps you lost sight of your greatness through your journey in life. Without a mentor you made mistakes and wandered away from your path of greatness. Perhaps you settled for less than who you are. It happens to many of us. You acquired responsibilities and then settled into a job that would pay the bills even if it may have been unfulfilling. You got yourself bogged down in a relationship that was conflicted but the price seemed too high to unwind it. Or perhaps you just stopped dreaming. Your life became a drudgery of getting by.

That is not who you are. Until you can see at least the spark of your greatness, you will have difficulty expanding it. Your greatness is meant to be your compass heading, your lighthouse, and your guide. You are meant to follow its path so that your greatness expands and overtakes all that is ordinary in your life.

We want to share some stories about seemingly ordinary people we know who are, nevertheless, rulers over their individual kingdoms.

These are people of greatness, dignity, and substance. We share their stories as an illustration because we hope you see your reflection in their faces. Any of these could be your story. Certainly, your story could be added to theirs.

Linda Linda works in the office of a nearby church. She doesn't care much about titles, material possessions, or being seen as special by others. Yet, there is an innocence to her that is otherworldly. Most people have armor, protection that has built up in reaction to the pain and difficulty of life. She has none. She radiates openness, honesty, and a genuine love for others. It is her greatness. Other people see it as well. They talk about how loving and helpful she is with everyone, every day. This is her gift to bring to the world. This is her kingdom over which she rules with goodness and grace.

John We met John many years ago. He put everything he had at risk in an experiment to create campus environments for retirees. It was his belief that senior citizens need an affordable retirement option that allows them to stay active, be involved, and socialize. His projects became the model for retirement communities across the country. He became wealthy. But, that wasn't how he was a great king. When he walked through the community, he knew everyone's name and they knew his. He cared for each person and for their welfare. He knew everything about his communities—down to how many dishes should be stacked on each shelf and the best temperature for the pools. He had created Camelot for elderly people. They were blessed by his vision and his care. In this way, he was a great king.

Diana Diana led a sales team for a major company. She was a focused, extremely hard-working, and demanding leader. She produced results. Her team hit its numbers year after year. She was very good at her job. But her greatness shined through when she had to lay people off for the first time. As she announced the layoff to her team she began to cry. It was obvious to everyone that this was one of the most difficult things she had ever done because she loved every one of her people. It was her love for her people that was her greatness. She watched over them, protected them, and encouraged them. Her people thrived under her leadership.

We could go on and on. These stories are endless. And they aren't about people who are typically glorified in books or in the media. They are stories about people like you and us: seemingly ordinary people who can be extraordinarily great.

Can you see the greatness in yourself? Can you see that you have a story similar to theirs? It is so important that you clearly see your greatness. It may appear in some little thing that truly matters to you. You may be moved to stand up for someone who is being bullied. You might find yourself giving a dollar to someone who is homeless. You might notice how tenderly you love your child. You might be working an extra job because you want your family to have some stability. Wherever you see the depth of your love or your nobility, you will find the seeds of your greatness. Greatness comes from the intersection of the spiritual world with the material one. Wherever you are the conduit for goodness and grace in the world, you become great.

Picture 3: Don't Worry, Be Happy!

You know you are leaning into your greatness when your days are filled with joy and fun. Happiness is the emotional indicator of being on the right path. Similarly, frustration, irritation, resentment, and unhappiness are all signs of being off the path of your greatness. Perhaps one of the greatest seductions and deceits in life is the willingness to endure unhappiness in the hope of a better situation in the future. You simply don't properly estimate the damage done to your being by living in negativity. It is toxic soil for your soul. Unhappiness is the warning bell that tells you of the need for a change. It is not worth working in a job you dislike because it pays well. It is not worth staying in a contentious relationship because you are afraid of being alone. It is not wise to deprive yourself now to save all you can to secure your future.

A dear friend of ours traveled to Ethiopia to spend time with his daughter who was serving a year as a missionary. Ethiopia is as poor a country as he had found. Riding through the capital city, he passed a lot filled with animal bones and vultures tearing at whatever scraps the butchers had missed. The smell was awful. Packs of children surrounded him everywhere begging for whatever he might give.

Meat, covered with flies, was sold from open stalls. The people lived in small huts with a simple fire in the middle.

Yet, despite their abject poverty, he had not found a people with greater joy. These people who had nothing radiated a goodness and grace that was infectious. Despite having almost nothing, everyone welcomed him and his daughter into their homes and shared the very best portion of whatever they were serving. How could it be that people who had so little material wealth possessed such a peace and joy?

Happiness is crucial to greatness. Happiness is evidence that you are living the life that belongs to you. It is the sign that you are honoring your balance. Happiness is a richness that can be shared endlessly without depleting you in the least.

We challenge you to live today with happiness as your guide. Ask yourself if you are happy right now. What is making you happy? What is limiting your happiness? What can you change to make yourself happier? Are you willing to make the change? If not, what is more important than your happiness? Why? Experiment with making small changes and notice the impact on your life.

Picture 4: Fill Your Life with Meaning and Purpose

Viktor Frankl (Frankl 1959) was a Jewish psychiatrist imprisoned in the Nazi concentration camps. He noticed that some prisoners seemed to endure their suffering and deprivation much better than did others. It was perplexing because it wasn't necessarily the physically strong who were able to sustain themselves under such wretched conditions. He found the true key to survival was maintaining a sense of meaning and purpose. Those who lost track of meaning and purpose deteriorated quickly, lost hope, and succumbed. Those who found ways to preserve and feed meaning and purpose were able to endure their suffering without it breaking their spirit.

So profound was this insight, Frankl used it as the basis of a new approach to psychotherapy that he called "Logo therapy." He was convinced that meaning and purpose are just as significant for thriving in ordinary life as they were in the prison camp. Regular people, like you and me, need to have a sense of purpose to make sense of our lives. He writes, "Man's search for meaning is the primary motivation in his life. . . . This meaning is unique and specific in that it must and can be fulfilled by him alone; only then does it achieve a significance that can satisfy his own will to meaning."

Could meaning be so important in your life? How is it that the poor can be so rich and the rich can be so poor?

It might be easy to attribute the difference to background, opportunity, economics, or circumstance, but there are simply too many rags to riches stories of people who emerged from the worst of circumstances to live amazing lives to not seek some deeper and more fundamental factor.

Could it be true that those who expand their Circles have found the pathway of true life meaning?

NFL star Jason Brown quit playing football professionally and now spends his days as a farmer who harvests free food for the hungry.

Jason Brown was drafted by the Baltimore Ravens in the fourth round of the 2005 National Football League draft and played college football at North Carolina. On February 28, 2009, Brown signed a five-year deal with the St. Louis Rams that was worth $37.5 million and included a $20 million guarantee. At the time, the deal made Brown the highest paid center in the NFL. On March 12, 2012, he was released by the Rams and decided to take his life in a new direction.

After he left football, Brown purchased a 1,030-acre farm near Louisburg, North Carolina, where he harvests food for the hungry.

Last weekend, Brown gave away 46,000 pounds of sweet potatoes, in addition to the 10,000 pounds of cucumbers that he has already given away.

"You look over a sweet potato field and you don't see a crop, the vines are kind of wilting. There is nothing there to pick. You've got to have faith. I went out to plow up the potatoes last week and looked behind the tractor. I don't know if I've ever seen anything quite as beautiful as those big brown potatoes lying everywhere," Brown told a local journalist.

Brown made a choice. He had become great in the world's eyes by becoming the highest paid center in the NFL. He certainly didn't need money. He could have easily milked his sports career for many years and then gone on the speaker's circuit to tell football war stories throughout the country.

Instead, he bought a farm. Perhaps he liked a rural life and looked forward to kicking back on a wide porch, sipping a drink, and watching the sun set. No, he is on a tractor cultivating, sowing, and reaping. Not for the money. Not because he needs the food but to give it away. He chose greatness. He dramatically expanded the impact of his life beyond that of his football career. He is creating ripples of goodness in the world that will go on for a very long time and may expand exponentially.

Who knows who his food will feed? Perhaps one of those people will go on to cure cancer or solve global warming. Or, perhaps one of the mouths he feeds will remember his gift and will pass it on by sharing with those who have less. Jason is changing the world. He is a truly rich man.

Your life, too, has meaning, even if you don't always recognize it. Things matter to you. You get out of bed every day for a reason. You may not have given much thought to those things that deeply matter to you, but you should. The more clearly you understand that which gives your life meaning, the more fully you can align yourself with it. Your greatness shows up in the things that deeply matter to you (Hartman 2014).

Chapter 16

Conclusion

At the start of our journey together through this book, we asked one simple question: Are you as happy as you would like to be? We believe it is your right to shine, to thrive, to live a life of purpose and meaning that makes you truly and deeply satisfied. Our goal has been both to provide you with insights into how to achieve the thriving level of happiness you so richly deserve as well as to inspire you to seek your greatness—we have done so by highlighting how to grow and balance your Circle. We hope we have done both and prompted you to think some new thoughts and to feel your heart and soul expand. Our bigger hope is that you will have taken a deliberate step to grow in your greatness.

As we reach the end of our journey through this book, we hope our journey together continues. We hope the Circle provides a tool for you to continually assess yourself and take steps toward thriving. Remember, the great people we admire—those who truly seem to be thriving—are only ordinary people who drew a big Circle for their lives. That Circle required them to become the thriving person they became. How did they do it, we might ask?

The path to a full and satisfying life begins by identifying what is and isn't important to you. What is important is in your Circle. Whatever is outside your Circle is not. Your life won't be any bigger or any richer than the size and content of your Circle. If you want more impact in your life, or more of a sense of satisfaction, or more peace and happiness, all you need to do is expand your Circle.

When you do, your world will change. You will think different thoughts, care about different things, and see the world around you in a bigger and more profound way.

But simply expanding what matters to you is not enough. You must also master the basic building blocks of greatness: independence, power, humility, and purpose. You must value your uniqueness highly enough that you are unwilling to conceal it or try to modify it in order to get along with the people in your life. Only then will you have the freedom to see, embrace, and cultivate your unique gift. Freeing yourself from your ego will allow you to truly experience how intimately you belong to every other human being on the face of the earth. It is the compassion born from humility that provides the motivation to see how your gift was meant to be best utilized for the good of others—your purpose.

The journey toward thriving never ends. Every step along the path is rich with wonder, power, and joy. And this path toward greatness is for everyone, regardless of your education, race, or level of outward success.

We have enjoyed sharing the wisdom we have gained from our journey with you and we encourage you to share yours with us. There are many who accept being ordinary as good enough. You are willing to step out of the crowd to take the sometimes-lonely road toward being extraordinary. We invite you to share your stories and experiences with us as we become a community of those who are seeking the greatness in ourselves and adding to the goodness in the world around us.

References

Agrawal, AJ. 2015. "4 Stories About Work Ethic That Will Make You Work Harder," *Inc.*, March 21. https://www.inc.com/aj-agrawal/4-stories-about-work-ethic-that-will-make-you-work-harderer.html.

Covey, Stephen R. 1989. *7 Habits of Highly Effective People*. New York: Simon & Schuster.

Frankl, Victor. 1959. *Man's Search for Meaning*. Boston: Beacon Press.

Gerber, Hestie Barnard. 2013. "10 Modern-Day Heroes Actively Changing the World." ListVerse, May 31. http://listverse.com/2013/05/31/10-modern-day-heroes-actively-changing-the-world/.

Hartman, Steve. 2014. "Why a Star Football Player Traded NFL Career for a Tractor." www.cbsnews.com/news/former-nfl-player-farms-for-good/.

Jobs, Steve. 2005. "'You've Got to Find What You Love,' Jobs Says." Commencement address, Stanford University, June 15. http://news.stanford.edu/news/2005/june15/jobs-061505.html.

Sutton, Robert. 2007. *The No Asshole Rule: Building a Civilized Workplace and Surviving One That Isn't*. New York: Warner Business Books.

Taylor, Jane. "The Violet." www.poetrysoup.com/famous/poem/3293/The_Violet.

Wikipedia. "Narcissus (mythology)." https://en.wikipedia.org/wiki/Narcissus_(mythology).

Williamson, Marianne. 1996. *A Return to Love*. New York: HarperCollins.

Index